Single Life

Being Your Best for God
As He Prepares His Best for You

Earl D. Johnson, Ph.D.

PNEUMA LIFE

PUBLISHING

Single Life

Earl D. Johnson, Ph.D.

Unless otherwise noted, Scripture quotations are taken from the New International Version. Copyright 1973, 1978, 1984, International Bible Society. Scripture quotations marked KJV are from the King James Version of the Bible. Scripture quotations marked Amplified are taken from the Amplified Old Testament, copyright 1962, 1964, Zondervan Publishing House and from the Amplified New Testament, copyright 1954, 1958, The Lockman Foundation. Verses marked TLB are taken from The Living Bible, copyright 1971, owned by assignment by Illinois Marine Bank N.A. (as trustee).

Printed in the United States of America
ISBN: 1-56229-427-X

Pneuma Life Publishing
P. O. Box 10612
Bakersfield, CA 93389
(805) 324-1741

Contents

Introduction

For years I've been embroiled in a semantic war over the word "single," especially among unmarried Christians. Recently, however, I discovered a definition for the term that contradicts most of what I have read throughout my life. The word "single" originates from the Greek word *heis*, meaning once for all, unique, unanimous, one of many, or only one. With such a diverse list of definitions, how has this term taken on such a negative connotation?

Frankly, I believe too little attention has been given to understanding single life as it is lived from the single's perspective. Theologians, church leaders, and well-meaning married Christians use Bible-banging tactics that leave an interminable trail of "thou-shalt-nots" for the single Christian to follow. The results have often left the Christian single utterly frustrated.

I've made a sincere effort to understand single life and the factors that affect it, such as loneliness, anxiety, and the fear of not ever marrying. This contributed to discovering the difference between males and females, their wants and desires, their opinions about our culture, and the stigma of being excluded from the "couples society."

The complex subject of singles has forced me and other church leaders to abandon previous unproven beliefs about singles — especially the notion that singles are automatically happy just because they are single. The growing singles population in the Church has forced us to take a serious look into the various categories of singles: young singles, older singles, divorced singles, widowed singles, and single heads of households. Church leadership must decide what to do about this burgeoning group and the unique challenges that they face.

This book is targeted to speak to the single person, but it is not merely a book about the single life. It is intended to give singles practical instruction in righteousness and how they can become joined to the whole Body of Christ. It is not meant for condemnation or judgment but offers the opportunity to look at the single life from the paradigm of the single in Christ.

Designed as a reference guide for singles, these pages will both challenge and help singles to cultivate godly living. It will also serve as a manual for church leadership who are seeking to nurture, train, and eventually utilize the singles population in their churches. Finally, it is a guide for marrieds seeking to identify and resolve issues from their single life and to go on to discover their own "uniqueness in Christ." Once that uniqueness is discovered, they will go on to be fruitful spouses in marriage.

This book focuses on the uniqueness of the unmarried. Often under-utilized in the church, singles can be a tremendous source of strength, leadership, and are, in fact, an extension of care to the other sheep in the fold. Properly trained and nurtured, the unmarried population will be accused of "turning the city upside down."

We need intensive training programs for singles to win the world. How I long to see every struggling single transformed into a dynamic servant who passionately shares Jesus with a dying world. Perhaps this smells of radicalism — but what are the alternatives? The church's unmarried population must exchange the world's pursuit of happiness for a sense of divine purpose and mission.

I trust this book will help to broaden the understanding of church leaders and encourage them to embrace the tremendous wealth of gifts, talent, and creativity resident in the single population of our churches. I pray that married Christians will not only empathize with their single brothers and sisters but minister grace, compassion, and love in the family of God. Finally, may these pages produce hope, courage, and a desire for excellence in the life of every single believer.

The principles found in this book pose great challenges: a challenge to give yourself totally to God; a challenge to trust Him more than you trust your own emotions; and a challenge to apply principles of godly living that will conform you into the image of Jesus Christ. May you find abundant grace to be a "doer of the Word" as you live as a single.

Chapter 1

A Time to Celebrate!

Many believers ride an emotional roller coaster during their single years. The never-married, divorced, and widowed grapple with a variety of emotions. Anxiety over meeting monthly bills. Anger over divorce proceedings and alimony. Gnawing emptiness when a husband or wife dies. Fear of never marrying — or never marrying again.

I know one young woman who wanted, more than anything else, to find and marry the man of her dreams. When this didn't happen, she sunk into chronic discouragement. Like many single believers, she was initially excited about her walk with God but became discouraged when it did not produce the expected results — a life partner.

Jesus offers all believers — regardless of their marital status — life more abundantly. When Jesus is truly Lord of our lives, we experience a full, satisfying, and purposeful life. His Lordship transcends every trial, difficulty, and circumstance. His work in our lives leads to love, peace, joy, righteousness, prosperity, and gladness.

Yet, the mood of our age, especially among singles, reflects the pursuit of a pseudo-abundant life created by the media. The movie and television standards of love and happiness set us up for disappointment. Who hasn't longed to experience "love at first sight"? How many women still wait for their knight in shining armor to carry them off to a life of bliss?

Real life is not what you see in Hollywood. The Christian single must set aside the worldly view of love and relationships. Life in the kingdom should be accompanied by a renewed, godly perspective.

Don't copy the behavior and customs of this world, but be a new and different person with a fresh newness in all you do and think. Then you will learn from your own experience how his ways will really satisfy you (Romans 12:2, TLB).

Nowhere is this new attitude needed more than in a single's knowledge of his or her love, acceptance, and self-image before God.

Right Desires

Singles must be convinced that God's love for them remains constant regardless of what does or does not happen in their lives.

Who shall separate us from the love of Christ? Shall trouble or hardship or persecution or famine or nakedness or danger or sword? . . . No, in all these things we are more than conquerors through him who loved us. For I am convinced that neither death nor life, neither angels or demons, neither the present nor the future, nor any powers, neither height nor depth, nor anything else in all creation, will be able to separate us from the love of God that is in Christ Jesus our Lord (Romans 8:35,37-39).

If you remain single for another five years, God still loves you. If you never marry, His love for you hasn't waned. Divorce, bereavement, or aching loneliness can't separate you from His care and concern.

When we understand God's love for us, we can humbly abandon our hopes and dreams, deferring them to His wisdom and counsel and believing totally in His faithfulness.

Learning the reality of God's love is the application point of this verse: "Be delighted with the Lord. Then he will give you all your heart's desires. Commit everything you do to the Lord. Trust him to help you do it and he will" (Psalm 37:4,5, TLB).

Most of us, at one time or another, have tenaciously claimed these verses as the basis for hanging on to our hopes and dreams. Unfortunately, we often skip the prerequisite of being delighted in the Lord. Instead we focus on God giving us the desires of our heart.

God, in His wisdom, knows our hearts are deceitfully wicked. Many of our hopes and dreams are based upon the misguided ambitions of our hearts. God wants to give us right desires in accordance with His plan for our lives.

A Different Kind of Love

What is love? God is love! If a person doesn't know God, how will he know love? First Corinthians 13 defines godly love and tells us what love does and doesn't do.

Love is very patient and kind, never jealous or envious, never boastful or proud, never haughty or selfish or rude. Love does not demand its own way. It is not irritable or touchy. It does not hold grudges and will hardly even notice when others do it wrong. It is never glad about injustice, but rejoices whenever truth wins out. If you love someone you will be loyal to him no matter what the cost. You will always believe in him, always expect the best of him, and always stand your ground in defending him (1 Cor. 13:4-7, TLB).

We must learn that love is love all the time. There is not one love for marriage and a different love for people in the church. Yes, there are degrees of love, but they all stem from the same source.

There is not one kind of love that courts and another that becomes evident upon marriage. God's love is different from the world's love. His standards for marriage are different from those of the justice of the peace or the wedding chapel in Las Vegas. God's standards and our perception of love must be in agreement before He can do the work in us He desires.

Worldly love calls for proof of its existence, requiring you to be always on stage, ready to perform.

God's standards are different. He performs for you. He provides for you. He cares for you.

"We love him because he first loved us.... And this commandment have we from him, That he who loveth God love his brother also" (1 John 4:19,21, KJV).

Love is responsive, not based on performance. The world invites you to try the merchandise for awhile; if you don't like it, return it for a refund or exchange.

Your love for each other (brothers and sisters in Christ, husbands, wives, mates-to-be) is directly linked to your commitment to love God. The Word says, "Taste and see that the Lord is good." The world says, "Taste and see if the object of your affection is good." In other words, relationships are based upon performance. Does this person meet my expectations? Is he or she to my liking?

The conditions of worldly love directly oppose the standards of God's love. We must abandon the world's standards and release the media fantasies of life hopes and dreams.

The Meat Market Syndrome

Far too many people marry an image rather than the person God desires for them. Our perceptions of worldly beauty play with the mind when God reveals His plan for us.

"Her? Why she is not my type at all. I'm a leg man!" a fellow might protest.

"Him? He doesn't resemble the man of my dreams!" a young lady might argue.

The child of God should never be suspended from a rack like a piece of beef or placed like a mannequin in a window for display. God doesn't want you to shop for a mate, either.

Dating, in the worldly sense, is nothing but a trial-and-error meat market experience. When it fails to work, the person is simply returned to the rack and another one is selected. No wonder dating is sometimes called the ministry of rejection. This should never happen in the Body of Christ!

Some Christians argue, "If they don't date, how will singles get to know each other?"

When considering a prospective mate, you should ask yourself, "Am I graced for this person, and is this person graced for me?"

Everything in God begins and ends in grace. A person's love for you is not, in itself, sufficient to make a marriage work. Only God's grace — His ability working through you — enables you to make adjustments, endure difficult moments, and tolerate selfish behavior.

When you abandon your images, God can pour His merciful love upon you and bring to you exactly what you need — and desire!

It boils down to one simple rule: You must completely trust that God's taste is agreeable with yours. How blessed is the one who concludes, "I don't want my way. I want the will of God for my life."

You're not the only one who has struggled with embracing God's will. God said to the children of Israel, "I do not want you to have a king. I am your God and will rule over you." History records that as soon as the Israelites passed through other lands and saw that the people were ruled by kings, they said to Samuel, "We want a king."

Wanting their own way led to immeasurable heartache, defeat in battle, and the eventual division of the kingdom.

Singles would do well to shun their own way and embrace God's will for their lives, especially in regard to their singleness.

God encourages single believers to seek first the kingdom of God. (See Matthew 6:33.) The emphasis of dating must never distract the single believer from the quest of "seeking the kingdom."

Eight Ways to Celebrate!

Being single offers the best time to prepare to celebrate unto the Lord! The apostle Paul asserts that the unmarried person cares for the things of the Lord, how he may please the Lord. (See 1 Cor. 7:32.) This verse characterizes the unmarried person as one with undivided devotion. This is a time of celebration, character development, and great love toward God.

The following suggestions will help you to form godly attitudes and opinions about your singleness. You can learn to celebrate this special time in your life.

1. Learn to understand and appreciate yourself. Discover your strengths and abilities, and thank God for them. Learning to live with and love yourself is one of the highest forms of acceptance that you can experience. Time spent appreciating yourself is an excellent investment.

2. *Find peace in being a believer.* Scripture tells us, "Seek peace and pursue it" (Psalm 34:14). Ridding yourself of fantasy only adds to your peace. Believing the "Prince Charming" syndrome or expecting "love at first sight" plays havoc, especially on women, and will only keep you in constant turmoil.

3. *Nurture friendships with both men and women that will enhance you.* People are the world's greatest resource. While you are single, surround yourself with people of both genders in order to bring intrinsic value to your own life. Knowing and interacting with others enhances your ability to love and be open.

4. *Structure your life so that behavior now will dictate behavior in future years.* Whatever you allow now will determine your future. If you do not correct certain thought patterns or behaviors when you discover them, they eventually will become ingrained in your life. Good or bad, you will be either the victim of them because of the negative or the recipient of them because of the good.

5. *While anticipating a life-partner, work on being fully developed and mature.* Use this time to set goals and actively pursue them.

Hope and expectation are passive. Goals are active. While there is nothing wrong with having a dream, you can't live by it alone. You need goals that give life direction and action. Pursuing your goals gives purpose to everything you do. Don't put your life on hold waiting for marriage. You can celebrate now!

6. *Learn patience and let it prove you in every area of your life.* "The patient in spirit is better than the proud in spirit" (Eccl. 7:8, KJV). Allowing patience to work in you brings good results. "But

you must let your endurance come to its perfect product, so that you may be fully developed and perfectly equipped, without any defects" (James 1:4, Williams New Testament).

7. *Get involved in helping someone else achieve a goal.* Sow your life into another person, preferably someone of the same gender, for an extended period of time. One of the best ways to accomplish this is through discipleship. A special joy awaits those who help others achieve goals and obtain new levels of commitment.

8. *Set at least three areas of goals, and set benchmarks for achieving them.* Let these goals, unlike the goals mentioned above, be structured so as to continue even if you were to marry. I refer to goals such as purchasing a home, enrolling in school to pursue a higher level of education, and setting zeniths for spiritual growth and development.

Do's and Don'ts

Notice that I did not mention "finding a mate" in my list of eight ways to celebrate. Why? I'll let the apostle Paul explain. Himself a single, Paul made some strong statements regarding singleness and marriage. Let's look at his perspective:

> Brother, each man, as responsible to God, should remain in the situation God called him to. Now about virgins: I have no command from the Lord, but I give a judgment as one who by the Lord's mercy is trustworthy. Because of the present crisis, I think that it is good for you to remain as you are. Are you married? Do not seek a divorce. Are you unmarried? Do not look for a wife. But if you do marry, you have not sinned; and if a virgin marries, she has not sinned. But those who marry will face many troubles in this life, and I want to spare you this (1 Cor. 7:24-28).

I found myself reading this passage in reverse order. Verse 28 asserts that a person commits no sin if he or she marries, but they are going to have a difficult time coping with the trials of life and adjusting to marriage at the same time. Verse 27 makes an emphatic statement: If you are married, don't seek a divorce. If you are single, don't seek a wife.

The conclusions of these two verses are based on the facts presented in verse 26:

I think then, because of the impending distress (that is even now setting in), it is well — expedient, profitable, and wholesome — for a person to remain as he or she is (1 Cor. 7:26, Amplified).

Our "impending distress" is not the lack of men for women, as the world would have you believe. Recent statistics state, "One in every three young black men in California is in prison, jail, or on probation or parole." The figure exceeds the one-in-four rate cited in national studies. It is not merely a shortage — it is gross disobedience!

The report noted that while one in every three young black men — totalling 67,556 — was in the criminal justice system, the rate was one in 19 young white males for 64,819 and one in 11 for 11,311 Latinos. [1]

The impending distress is the mentality of a troubled world that emphasizes man-made solutions over the wisdom of God. Singles should not lean to their own understanding or worldly wisdom. They must keep looking to God, trusting in His ability to provide for their needs.

Father Knows Best

A young child does not question the guidance of his parents. As he explores the world around him, however, he begins to test their judgment. Confidence in his own ability to discover things for himself, the very trait that led to man's original fall, leads him astray.

When he sees a beautiful object beyond the boundaries his parents have set, he rebels. In fact, he develops a distrustful attitude because he thinks something good is being withheld from him. Of course, we know that loving parents set boundaries for the protection of their children.

A child often becomes intent on breaking the rules and challenging boundaries — until he reaps some stinging consequences. Burning a finger on a hot stove or getting shocked by an electrical outlet makes a powerful impression. Maybe my parents are smarter than I think, he concludes.

We must become like that little child, absolutely confident that Father knows best! Perfect in all knowledge and wisdom, God knows exactly how to care for us.

Scripture teaches that God often births a vision or desire in our hearts and then brings death to it. During this time, our faith is challenged and strengthened. We also yield our selfish ambitions and impure motives to God. If it is still His will, God miraculously resurrects this vision and provides divine power to bring it to fulfillment.

Many of God's servants experienced a death to their visions. God promised Abraham a son, but He allowed 25 years to pass before Isaac's birth.

God gave Joseph a dream of ruling over his father, mother, and brothers. Sold into slavery, falsely accused, and thrown into prison, Joseph's vision died an excruciating death. Eventually, however, he interpreted Pharaoh's dreams and became overseer of the land during a terrible famine. In danger of starvation, his brothers bowed down to him and requested grain to keep their families alive.

The prophet Samuel anointed David to be king over Israel, but for years the shepherd and sweet singer of songs fled before the mad King Saul. His hope of ever becoming king was repeatedly dashed.

The struggles that accompany our natural aspirations are absent in the resurrected vision. You may choose to subscribe to this teaching, or simply choose to give things over to God because He knows best. Whatever your decision, you must rid yourself of the responsibility of looking out for your own interests.

Trust God for every desire of your heart, even the desire for a life partner. If you lean on the counsel of God, His Word will begin to work in you. Allow your hopes and dreams to be rooted and grounded in Him. When we abandon our own hopes and dreams in favor of God's perfect plan for our lives, we defer to His wisdom and trust in His faithfulness.

Chapter 2

Don't Give Yourself Away

"It's been so long since I've been with a man that I'm looking for someone to give myself away to," one woman confided to another. Unfortunately, remarks such as this are heard far too often among Christian singles. Because they fail to understand God's purpose in sexual abstinence, singles often lapse into frustration and discouragement, leading to bad decisions in their relationships.

Having been intimately involved with a handsome young man, a Christian woman suffered pangs of regret: "As believers we vowed to abstain from sexual activity, so I never went to bed with him. When we broke up, however, I still felt violated because of the heavy petting that we had done."

God intended this woman to be a gift to her future husband. She and her boyfriend, however, had begun to untie the ribbons and rumple the wrapping paper. She had given away part of herself emotionally and physically to this young man.

Abstinence is not merely keeping yourself from premarital intercourse; it is also guarding your emotions from being violated. It is not "seeing how far we can go without going all the way." Carrying yourself as a gift into marriage infers that you will go into that relationship free from the condemnation of a horrible past, physically or emotionally.

The pastor of a church in London gave this helpful formula: "If you are not going to partake of the main meal, don't mess around with the hors d'oeuvres." Sex before marriage is hors d'oeuvres!

God calls us to purity, which is a much higher standard than virginity. Many Christian singles engage in kissing, hugging, and more intimate forms of touching before marriage. You can do a lot and still remain a technical virgin.

Asking "How far is too far?" reveals a heart bent toward sin. You need to ask, "What is pleasing to God?" Respect yourself — and members of the opposite sex.

Sexual sin and broken relationships burden many singles with emotional pain. That's why I ask them, "Are you free from sexual bondage now and do you carry into marriage yourself as a gift to your partner?"

My brother put it this way in a sermon: "If the Holy Spirit cannot keep you when you are single, how will a husband or wife keep you when you are married?"

Why Practice Abstinence?

Celibacy, in the biblical sense, is never accomplished as a work of the flesh. It must result from a life of dedication to the Lord. Celibacy springs from a desire to please Christ — not just to follow religious rules. "And whatsoever ye do in word or deed, do all in the name of the Lord Jesus.... And whatsoever ye do, do it heartily, as to the Lord, and not unto men" (Col. 3:17,23, KJV).

When a person practices abstinence merely because he believes it is expected, he performs a work of the flesh. On the other hand, when the person abstains because of God's unconditional love for him, he is motivated by love and performs a work of the spirit.

Abstinence is simply a matter of developing self-control — a fruit of the spirit — rather than self-denial, which is a work of the flesh. Self-control and its accompanying fruit are part of God's covenant with the believer. The single walks in the covenant of love rather than in a legalistic abstinence as a work of the flesh.

> For this is the will of God, even your sanctification, that ye should abstain from fornication: that every one of you should know how to possess his vessel in sanctification and honour; not in the lust of concupiscence, even as the Gentiles which know not God (1 Thess. 4:3-5, KJV).

What's the motivation for living a pure life? Knowing God. You've undoubtedly heard many sermons about abstaining from sexual sin. More often than not, ministers deliver these messages in the spirit of compulsion and not of love.

Spiritual obedience demands two elements — love of God and fear of God.

When we understand God's love for us and respond accordingly, this reality becomes ours: "Being confident of this very thing, that he which hath begun a good work in you will perform it until the day of Jesus Christ" (Phil. 1:6, KJV).

Jesus warmly invites us into obedience: "If you love me, you will obey what I command" (John 14:15). Loving God and fearing Him result in an ability to present your body as a living sacrifice to the Lord. Jesus gave you a new life. He gave you a new conscience and a new desire — a desire to possess your body in sanctification and honor. God intends celibacy to be a celebration unto Him — a rejoicing. It celebrates the death of the flesh through Jesus Christ and the resurrection of life in Him!

Scripture points us to this very fact: "Dearly beloved, I beseech you as strangers and pilgrims, abstain from fleshly lusts, which war against the soul" (1 Peter 2:11, KJV). Do not engage in private wars. Abstain from fleshly lusts. Give yourself to a life of holiness and righteousness to the Lord!

A Happy Ending

One woman, in her own words, describes how she grappled with the challenge of being single:

"While still in high school, I fell in love with a man four years my senior. I considered myself to be a good girl, so I refused to be sexually involved with him. He didn't push the issue. I was so proud to be able to keep him without compromising my values.

"I'd been taught that sex before marriage was wrong. If a young man loved me, he would wait. I felt sure this was the person I would spend the rest of my life with. I was very happy, but my bliss was short-lived. He broke off our relationship and told me that he would be marrying someone else because she was having his baby! He even invited me to his wedding.

"The marriage didn't last. He separated from his wife a few months after the baby was born. Two years later he was back in my life. Thinking I could recapture what we had lost, I allowed myself to fall in love again. Rather than risk losing him, I began to have sex with him.

"Eventually, I got pregnant. Much to my dismay, he told me he was also dating another woman — and he thought she, too, might be pregnant! I had been expecting a proposal but was disappointed when he said, 'As soon as my divorce is final, I will marry you. But I can't just walk out on this other woman. I want you to understand that up front.'

"What nerve! Not wanting to settle for such an arrangement, I broke off our relationship, leaving me devastated, unwed, and pregnant! More than anything else, I was humiliated and mad.

"Instead of acknowledging my sin for having sex outside of marriage, I transferred most of the blame to him, labeling him a no-good philanderer. I also condemned myself for being too stupid to see it. I vowed never to allow myself to be hurt by a man again.

"About a year and a half later, I met and married a wonderful man. Unfortunately, I brought all my hurt into this marriage. My attitude toward my husband was, 'I love you, but I don't need you!' and I regularly let him know it in no uncertain terms. We had a stormy marriage for ten miserable years because I was incapable of wholly submitting myself to him as a wife. I truly believed my 'independence' was crucial to my survival.

"We both agreed that it was impossible to continue the relationship and decided to call it quits. After a three-month separation, I realized that I did indeed love this man — and he loved me. We decided to try again. Without any solutions in sight, all we had was a dogged determination to 'stick it out.'

"That's when the Lord began an inner healing in me. He showed me that my inability to trust and, therefore, my inability to love, resulted from not forgiving the man who had previously hurt me. God showed me how I had felt the need to 'point the finger' at someone else to cover my own sin because I had never forgiven myself. I had blamed this former boyfriend and built a protective shield over my heart so I could live with my guilt.

"Jesus asked me to acknowledge my own sin and to give Him the hurt that I had carried for so long. He promised me that I would be free to love my husband as He intended, which was what I so desperately desired.

"I had to stop blaming my husband. Although he was not without fault in our relationship, that was not where my wounds originated.

"Jesus taught me the very same lesson that David learned from his sin with Bathsheba and his attempt to cover it up. "There was a time when I wouldn't admit what a sinner I was. But my dishonesty made me miserable and filled my days with frustration.... My strength evaporated like water on a sunny day until I finally admitted all my sins to you and stopped trying to hide them" (Psalm 32:3-5, TLB).

"Not only was I suffering from guilt, but I had developed a poor self-image as well. Having failed in this past relationship, I didn't think much of myself as a person. I built a strong, independent facade around my hurt ego to hide from the world what I really believed I was — a failure!

"If you think you are no good, you will be no good to yourself and others. You have to be true to yourself. Stand firm in what you believe. If you fail, get up, shake the dust off, let Jesus heal your hurts, and press on! Even though you might lose a relationship because of your convictions, you will ultimately reap the reward of God's best for you.

"My story has a happy ending, but my husband and I — and our children — suffered a lot of agony. When I allowed Jesus to heal my wounds from the past, I was freed from the self-induced bondage that was destroying my marriage. I am now free to totally trust God for a healed and growing marriage. It's not without bumps — no marriage is — but I know it will survive and thrive because Jesus is in its center. He put our marriage together, and He will hold it together."

This woman's testimony proves you can trade in your bitterness for the sweet healing touch of Jesus. He will teach you to be realistic about your past, enabling you to use those harsh experiences as solid stepping stones to a promised future. (See Jer. 29:11.)

Forgiveness is a key to wholeness. We must release the past and those who have hurt us in order to build a positive self-image in Christ. As long as we keep an unforgiving spirit, our self-image is formed through our perception of what those who hurt us thought us to be and not what Christ says we are.

You must realize that unless you are "whole," you cannot experience a positive union with another.

The apostle Paul gives good advice to anyone who has suffered hurt: "And have no fellowship with the unfruitful works of darkness, but rather reprove them" (Eph. 5:11, KJV). The NIV tells us to "have nothing to do with the fruitless deeds of darkness, but rather expose them."

In other words, don't fellowship with your past hurts and disappointments because you are now children of light. Stop commiserating with your hurts and unresolved inner conflicts (pity parties). Expose them and be healed of them.

Discontinue your fellowship with fruitless thoughts, deeds, and people. Prepare a celebration unto the Lord by identifying and dealing with the hurts of the past. Refuse to allow them to compound on those you undoubtedly will encounter later.

Released from the Past

The inability to put away their past hinders many singles from realizing their full potential in Christ. How can you cut off the influence of your old sins, previous relationships, and ungodly attitudes?

God gave the Israelites specific instructions on conquering their enemies. We can apply the principles to our lives today.

When the Lord thy God shall bring thee into the land whither thou goest to possess it, and hath cast out many nations before thee.... And when the Lord thy God shall deliver them before thee; thou shalt smite them, and utterly destroy them; thou shalt make no covenant with them, nor shew mercy unto them: Neither shalt thou make marriages with them; thy daughter thou shalt not give unto his son, nor his daughter shalt thou take unto thy son.... But thus shall ye deal with them; ye shall destroy their altars, and break down their images, and cut down their groves, and burn their graven images with fire (Deut. 7:1-3,5, KJV).

These principles, which every believer should adopt as his own, provide us with insight into the very heart of God who longs to give us victory.

1. When the Lord delivers you from past habits or anything that keeps you from being victorious, you must totally destroy your enemies (verse 2).

2. Make no agreements with your past (verse 2).

3. Do not marry the heathens of this world, or those who are opposed in lifestyle to the kingdom of God (verse 3). Your sons are not to marry their daughters; your daughters are not to marry their sons.

This is perhaps one of the most debated standards in the Church today. Even the apostle Paul agreed with this wisdom: "Do not be yoked together with unbelievers" (2 Cor. 6:14). We must confess that we do not understand all of God's ways, but we do know that He is righteous and just.

4. Tear down their altars, break down their images, and cut down their groves (verse 5). You must completely destroy anything that hinders your full devotion to God.

The Lord also told the Israelites to "neither make mention of the name of their gods" (Joshua 23:7, KJV). The names of the heathen's gods were not to be uttered from the lips of God's people.

Seek God's wisdom for applying these principles to your life.

What has God delivered you from? List your old sins, problems, former boyfriends or girlfriends. Now form a list of things that you should avoid to keep from going astray. God may want you to shun certain places or activities that might lead you to sin.

Has God set you free from pornography? If you want to stay free, don't linger near the magazine rack in convenience stores, supermarkets, or bookstores. Don't subscribe to Sports Illustrated just before the release of their annual swimsuit issue. Don't let cable TV entice you into becoming enslaved again to your former lusts.

No matter what the sin, you can totally destroy its power over you. Break its hold in the name of Jesus Christ. Exercise your God-given authority as a child of the Most High.

Make no agreement with things that previously ruled you. You were once in bondage to sin. When that bond is broken, sever all ties with practices that led you astray. Go on with God.

What's the inevitable result of acting on these principles? "Happy is that people, whose God is the Lord!" (Psalm 144:15, KJV). You can celebrate because it is well with you and your Creator. You have overcome the world by living according to God's standards.

Do You Need Emotional Healing?

If you fail to properly deal with hurt, especially as a result of broken relationships, it will only compound as you move into the deeper things of God. Don't deny the pain. God knew that you would be emotionally injured by others.

How can you know if you're really healed of past hurt? Jesus gave us a clue in the following verse:

. . . for the prince (evil genius, ruler) of the world is coming. And he has no claim on Me — he has nothing in common with Me, there is nothing in Me that belongs to him, he has no power over Me (John 14:30, Amplified).

Scripture provides us with a checklist for evaluating whether we have overcome the hurts of the past. They should have:

1. No claim on me.

2. Nothing in common with me.

3. Nothing in me that belongs to him.

4. No power over me.

Nothing. Wow! Ask yourself: Do I have unresolved issues in my heart and mind that Satan can manipulate? Have I completely moved away from his territory and left no forwarding address? Am I emotionally free?

I ministered for years under compounded hurt and pain, which produced insecurity and mistrust in me. I chose to ignore the pain and continued to minister to others. God's anointing seemed to be upon my life while, in fact, His grace was hovering over me to bring deliverance.

I persisted in suppressing the pain in my life rather than yielding to the sufficiency of the grace of God. Other hurting men and women must stop teaching about being healed until they allow the Holy Spirit to heal them in the name of Jesus. They must be the partakers of the fruit.

Unfortunately, much talk about healing has been merely a fad. We must begin practicing what we know about the Word of God and its ability to heal our hurts.

The Spirit of the Lord [is] upon Me . . . He has sent Me to announce release to the captives, and recovery of sight to the blind; to send forth delivered those who are oppressed — who are downtrodden, bruised, crushed, and broken down by calamity (Luke 4:18, Amplified).

Jesus began His ministry with a powerful declaration from Isaiah 61. If Jesus came to set you free, what hurt is more powerful than His ability to heal you? God desires to set you free from hurts incurred through broken relationships, trusted friends, and poor self-image.

When a person develops friendships, he or she places a priority on trust. When that trust is betrayed, hurt develops. Most people have not acquired the strength of overcoming that pain, so they withdraw from others and go inward. You must be healed in order to survive further relationships.

Hurt, disappointments, pain from past relationships, and unresolved inner conflicts dim your discernment about spiritual things.

What solution does God give us?

So that you may surely learn to sense what is vital, and approve and prize what is excellent and of real value — recognizing the highest and the best, and distinguishing the moral differences; and that you may be untainted and pure and unerring and blameless, that — with hearts sincere and certain and unsullied — you may [approach] the day of Christ, not stumbling nor causing others to stumble (Phil. 1:10, Amplified).

God honors His Word. You must still go to the cross to be healed of hurt, bitterness, and emotional pain inflicted by others. As healing comes, expect greater discernment, an increase in your ability to love, and emotional freedom in Christ.

Know Who You Are

Why are many single believers tempted to have premarital intimate relations? Because they lack positive self-identification. Many are embarrassed by who they are. Some are not even aware how valuable they are to God.

This passage from Deuteronomy represents God's special selection of the believer:

> For thou art an holy people unto the Lord . . . the Lord thy God hath chosen thee to be a special people unto himself, above all people that are upon the face of the earth. The Lord did not set his love upon you, nor choose you, because ye were more in number than any people . . . but because the Lord loved you . . . . He is God, the faithful God, which keepeth covenant and mercy with them that love him and keep his commandments . . . (Deut. 7:6-9, KJV).

You are special! You have been created in the image of God and possess tremendous potential. You are precious in His sight. He loves you with an everlasting love and will draw you to Himself. Celebrate His love in your life.

Celebrate God's mercy in your life. Though you were formerly alienated from God, He has brought you near through the blood of His Son. Shine and be splendid in His love for you. Celebrate His goodness in your life. Boast in the knowledge that He has received you as His child. Celebrate His acceptance and your special selection! Yes, celebrate your celibacy with singing, dancing, and thanksgiving.

When you understand your special selection, you can lean on it for your acceptance, security, and self-image. God is love, and He loves you with Himself. Celebrate your celibacy!

When You Blow It

If you experience a moral lapse, broken covenants of celibacy are reparable. The requirement, however, is for the believer to understand the power of the new life in Christ Jesus. God's ability to make new touches the spirit, soul, and body. God's power to make new goes beyond what men have done. In its place is His love and acceptance.

Life in the Spirit precludes mistakes. Repentance covers the mistake of having had an active sex life. True repentance means a turning away from, having a change of mind, and reversing one's direction. Do not be imprisoned by your past. When you appropriate the power of salvation in your life, you receive the resurrected and redemptive power of God.

In consulting those who work closely with singles (women in particular), I discovered that sexual sin is often only the manifestation of other maladies such as loneliness, insecurity, the need to be loved (touched, held, positively affirmed), and poor self-image.

Without proper ministry to correct these feelings, repentance is ineffective. Repentance may be genuine to the point of agreeing with God that an act is sinful and therefore hateful. If that repentance is ill-defined, however, it is ultimately ineffectual. Without understanding the root motivation for sinful behavior, how can one promise it will not be repeated?

Consider the following verses:

Search me, O God, and know my heart; test my thoughts. Point out anything you find in me that makes you sad, and lead me along the path of everlasting life (Psalm 139:23,24, TLB).

But how can I ever know what sins are lurking in my heart? Cleanse me from these hidden faults. And keep me from deliberate wrongs; help me to stop doing them. Only then can I be free of guilt and innocent of some great crime (Psalm 19:12,13, TLB).

It is not always the burning desire in their bodies that drives singles to commit sexual sin. A combination of factors may cause them to seek acceptance through sexual acts. The only remedy is the knowledge that God has already accepted them!

Not all sexual sin can be explained away by our assumptions. Those who lack self-control naturally tend toward sexual sin. But even disciplined singles struggle with the notion, "If God gave me these desires, why can't I express them?" This creates a dilemma for them, and they often lose sight of their purpose, goals, and destiny.

The key to understanding this is the biblical phrase, "in the fullness of time." God has some things on "time release."

Who Owns Your Body?

Singles can present their bodies to the Lord daily and find victory in doing so. Each day when you awake, present your body to God in this way:

Father, in the name of Jesus, I thank You that You are my Creator. You have made me in a wonderful way. I thank You for every emotion that You have given me to assist in understanding the world around me. I deem myself incapable of right emotional expression without Your help. Therefore, I present back to You every feeling that my body will experience. I sanctify myself to You and preserve my faculties holy unto You. I do this fully expecting that when the time for full release and expression arrives, You will continue to guide me in the proper expression of these emotions. Amen!

Even after praying this daily, some will still fall prey to sexual sin. When this happens, exercise your spiritual rights through the blood and the name of Jesus Christ to see yourself forgiven.

"Old things are passed away; behold, all things are become new" (2 Cor. 5:17, KJV). The definition for "new" is never before used, presented the first time, not old. Your life is new, your body is new, your consciousness is new. You can now walk in the power of this new life. Renew the covenant of celibacy with God.

These promises are not only for those who were sexually active before their salvation; it is also for those who have fallen into sexual sin after salvation. You can renew your covenant with God. You can receive forgiveness and shine again, be aglow with His glory, and know what it means to rejoice.

This is a good promise! Many people coming to the Lord have been victims of our permissive society. As part of proving their love, they have often engaged in sexual sins.

Resist the temptation to prove your love for a person. It is not a matter of making someone wait, but of presenting yourself as a marriage gift to your life partner.

As one young lady put it to an amorous young man, "Even if I wanted to give you my body, I cannot. It doesn't belong to me. I am bought with a price. I do not own my body."

Standing firmly on God's Word will enable you to reap great benefits, both now and in future relationships. You will be satisfied with the results and will be able to give all the glory to God.

Chapter 3

Running With Abandonment

Vince Lombardi said to his running backs, "Whenever you get the ball, run with abandonment." The single believer must pursue excellence in the same manner — with abandonment. Let nothing get in the way. Let nothing hinder you from the pursuit of your goals.

Excellence means possessing good qualities in an unusual degree. Thus, singles can use this time in their life to develop those good qualities. This means making sacrifices, re-arranging their schedules, and being capable of "feeling alone" for the sake of their goals.

How can we enjoy a life of excellence? Jesus told us to examine our focus. He said, "But seek ye first the kingdom of God, and his righteousness; and all these things shall be added unto you" (Matthew 6:33, KJV).

What does "first" mean to you? Does it mean after you've tried everything else? Of course not. Yet, often beset by pain from our own frustrated efforts, we beseech God for answers that will cure our malady instead of seeking the kingdom of God to ensure a healthy life.

He also is the Head of [His] Body, the church; seeing He is the Beginning, the First-born from among the dead, so that He alone in everything and in every respect might occupy the chief place —stand first and be pre-eminent (Col. 1:18, Amplified).

You must seek the kingdom of God before you seek anything else. He is life. He is peace. He is joy. He is the fulfillment of all your dreams. When you find Him, you have found all else. He must be first, reigning in your life above all else.

You've probably heard the saying, "If He cannot be Lord of all, He will not be Lord at all." While I believe the purpose of this statement, it needs to be clarified. Jesus is Lord all the time. Simply because you do not allow Him to be Lord of your life does not negate the fact that He is Lord.

You may admit that some areas of your life are outside His Lordship. You may doubt your ability to trust Him in everything, but He remains Lord. He is Lord whether situations in your life dictate that truth or not.

Desire the kingdom. Study the kingdom. Be active in seeking the kingdom. Be a "doer" of the Word, not just a "hearer" (James 1:22, KJV).

Scripture says, "For the kingdom of God is . . . righteousness, and peace, and joy in the Holy Ghost" (Romans 14:17, KJV). The Amplified Bible puts it another way. "[After all,] the kingdom of God is not a matter of [getting the] food and drink [one likes], but instead, it is righteousness . . . and heart-peace and joy in the Holy Spirit." Food and drink can mean getting our own desires met above that "which makes a person acceptable to God" (Romans 14:17b, Amplified).

So, since Christ suffered in the flesh [for us, for you], arm yourselves with the same thought and purpose [patiently to suffer rather than fail to please God]. For whoever has suffered in the flesh [having the mind of Christ] has done with [intentional] sin — has stopped pleasing himself and the world, and pleases God. So that he can no longer spend the rest of his natural life living by [his] human appetites and desires, but [he lives] for what God wills (1 Peter 4:1,2, Amplified).

The road to excellence is paved with blood, sweat, and tears, but what a celebration awaits those who persevere and refuse to settle for anything less.

Remember Jesus was willing to die a shameful death on the cross because of the joy He knew would be His afterwards; and now He sits in the place of honor by the throne of God. (See Hebrews 12:2.)

The same principle should apply to His children. The apostle Paul records:

And since we are his children, we will share his treasures — for all God gives to his Son Jesus is now ours too. But if we are to share his glory, we must also share his suffering. Yet what we suffer now is nothing compared to the glory he will give us later (Romans 8:17,18, TLB).

If God promised us a glorious future in eternity with Him, we should gratefully celebrate His goodness. Who can fully comprehend His mercy and grace? He has also promised to meet our every need. He delights in giving us the desires of our heart, having already decided that we should enjoy abundance in this life.

Determined to Know Him

The single person has the greatest opportunity in life to develop a solid relationship with God and understand the Lordship of Jesus.

[For my determined purpose is] that I may know Him — that I may progressively become more deeply and intimately acquainted with Him, perceiving and recognizing and understanding [the wonders of His Person] more strongly and more clearly. And that I may in that same way come to know the power outflowing from His resurrection [which it exerts over believers]; and that I may so share His sufferings as to be continually transformed [in spirit into His likeness even] to His death . . . (Phil. 3:10, Amplified).

As a single believer, what is your determined purpose? Understand that your life must go back to the life-giver. Plan and carry out a celebration unto the Lord each day as you present your body a living sacrifice unto Him.

The term "determined" means to settle, to fix, to establish. You must understand the cost of pursuing excellence. That cost could mean separation from friends, family, and others in order to accomplish what God has spoken to you.

The apostle Paul states that he would rather lose everything and win Christ. You must be willing to let everything else go in order to come to a place where you are doing things excellently and to the glory of God.

Note the term "perceiving and recognizing and understanding [the wonders of His Person]." This involves your time — time spent in the Word and communicating with Him. Then you will become more deeply and intimately acquainted with Him.

Don't feel guilty because your reason for following Jesus was the fish and the loaves. Marriage should not be the motivation behind following the Word or fellowship with God. Your determined purpose should be "to know Him . . ."

Make it your goal to become a potent, devil-hating, God-fearing single who understands what it means to be holy unto the Lord.

[Live] as children of obedience [to God]; do not conform yourselves to the evil desires [that governed you] in your former
ignorance [when you did not know the requirements of the
Gospel]. But as the One Who called you is holy, you yourselves also be holy in all your conduct and manner of living.
For it is written, You shall be holy, for I am holy (1 Peter 1:14-
16, Amplified).

Holiness is the way to celebrate excellence unto the Lord. To be
holy means to be separated for a particular use; for the exclusive
use of. The believer should, therefore, celebrate by being available
for God's exclusive use. In your life as a single, you have the unique
opportunity to be exclusive — just for Him!

Staying Focused

When Jesus healed the blind man, He asked him, "Do you see
anything?" (Mark 8:23). The man responded, "I see people; they
look like trees walking around." His answer indicated that he had
not received a complete healing. Jesus put His hands on the man's
eyes again, and his sight was restored, enabling him to see everything clearly.

When God finishes His work in you, you will have a complete
revelation of what He wants you to do. With a deeper insight into
who He is and how He proposes to use you, your completeness in
Christ will become a reality. You will understand you can do nothing in and of yourself, but that through Him you can do all things.
Hebrews 13:20,21 states:

Now the God of peace, that brought again from the dead our
Lord Jesus, that great shepherd of the sheep, through the blood
of the everlasting covenant, make you perfect in every good
work to do His will, working in you that which is wellpleasing
in his sight, through Jesus Christ; to whom be glory for ever
and ever. Amen (KJV).

Singles often thwart the development of attributes that cause them to excel, refraining from pushing themselves. Scripture encourages the single to "sense what is vital, and approve and prize what is excellent and of real value" (Phil. 1:10, Amplified).

This attitude focuses our energies, causing us to shun time-wasting activities and giving us greater spiritual discernment. A lack of discernment prevents us from celebrating excellence. If we are to excel, we must make an all-out effort to do what is necessary to excel.

This question should be asked of singles:

You were running a good race. Who cut in on you and kept you from obeying the truth?... The one who is throwing you into confusion will pay the penalty, whoever he may be (Gal. 5:7,10b).

One way to keep focused is to set goals for yourself. You may need to set realistic goals that will address the building and maintenance of character. Who you are is much more important to project than how you look or feel.

A teacher once defined "character" as "what you are when no one else is around." Building character must include developing a love for the Word of God and taking hold of those things that are necessary for character building from the Word.

You can only set realistic goals for life, work, and education if you have a realistic view of who you are. So much of our self-perception and how we see others comes from the conditioning we receive from television, magazines, and other mass media. Our character must be solely based on what God has said about us — not on what others perceive us to be or what we think of ourselves (positive or negative).

> I warn everyone among you not to estimate and think of himself more highly than he ought — not to have an exaggerated opinion of his own importance; but to rate his ability with sober judgment . . . (Romans 12:3, Amplified).

The key to building and maintaining character is to begin and end with sober judgment. The wise will avoid the quick-fix techniques of positive thinking. Instead, gird up your minds based solely upon what is revealed to you from the Word of God. Avoid the temptation to psyche yourself into things.

New Age and near-New Age thoughts proliferate in our day. In fact, some of the methods and principles that believers employ today for self-advancement border on New Age methods and principles.

Positive assertion without the grace of God is borderline New Age. Attempts at "inner healing" without the "inward witness" could be construed as New Age. Because these methods appear right, they are widely accepted in Christian circles. This acceptance gives a mixed message to onlookers. Those who purport to "defend" the faith have, in many instances, mislabeled this thrust as New Age.

This approach attempts to lower the worth of God and His Word in the lives of believers who are encouraged in the Word to be dependent upon God instead of what is inside of us. But the Word makes it clear that "every inclination of his [man's] heart is evil from childhood" (Gen. 8:21).

New Age thought and philosophy are vain deceit. Beware of attempting to build on such a foundation. You cannot build character aside from the inward work of the Holy Spirit.

> The heart is deceitful above all things and beyond cure. Who can understand it? I the Lord search the heart and examine the mind . . . (Jer. 17:9,10).

The process of building godly character begins with aligning your thoughts, intents, notions, actions, heart's desires, dreams, hopes, and aspirations with God.

Jesus told His disciples, "Apart from me you can do nothing" (John 15:5). True then; true now. You cannot do anything, be anything, or expect anything without Christ in your life.

Got an Attitude?

Let us embark upon the scriptural pathway to developing character. The Psalmist declared, "Your word is a lamp to my feet and a light for my path" (Psalm 119:105). Use the light of God's Word to scrutinize the pathways of life on which you travel.

Receive God's instructions, not as brow-beating from a man, but as your own personal revelation for godly living. God's Word is not some mystical set of rules that we could never successfully follow. Instead, He gives us clear and definitive steps to take as we celebrate life through His Living Word.

The following compilation of Bible verses will help you to develop and maintain godly character. The lamp unto your feet will show you where you are. The light unto your path will show you where to go.

Let's turn on the lamp and look at some of the warning signs the Word has posted on life's roads. The first step is to ascertain if, in fact, we are on the right road. Are we pursuing a celebration of excellence unto the Lord, or have we stumbled onto the wide and crowded road that leads to destruction?

As you examine these road signs, remember to be honest with yourself, yet fair. You don't need to wallow in despair if you discover you're on the wrong road. God has a crossroad just ahead that will take you in the right direction. Ask yourself these questions to determine if your attitudes are sending you in the right direction.

1. Am I guarding my heart, taking care of what I hear and allow to grow inside my spirit?

Listen and understand. What goes into a man's mouth does not make him "unclean," but what comes out of his mouth, that is what makes him "unclean."

... Don't you see that whatever enters the mouth goes into the stomach and then out of the body? But the things that come out of the mouth come from the heart, and these make a man "unclean." For out of the heart come evil thoughts, murder, adultery, sexual immorality, theft, false testimony, slander. These are what make a man "unclean" (Matt. 15:10,11, 17-20).

2. Am I watching my thoughts and cultivating life-producing thinking?

An unclean heart is devoid of understanding. Scripture declares that "the fear of the Lord is the beginning of wisdom" (Prov. 9:10). A heart that fears God will provide issues that are honest to ponder.

As a single person, don't let anyone condemn you when you begin to judge the fruit of young men and women who come into your life. If the fruit they produce matches the characteristics and deeds listed above, they are to be avoided! Guard your fellowship with people.

3. Am I pressured to go along with the crowd, or do I follow the Word deposited in my spirit?

Bad company corrupts good character (1 Cor. 15:33).

Evil communications corrupt good manners (1 Cor. 15:33, KJV).

Do not follow the crowd in doing wrong ... (Exodus 23:2).

Don't feel obligated to participate in activities that violate your human spirit. Sanctification is one of the expenses of pursuing what is excellent.

4. Am I compromising my standards regarding God's Word? Do I look for reasons to do it "my way"?

Be careful not to make a treaty with those who live in the land . . . or they will be a snare among you (Exodus 34:12).

Note David's level of repentance before God: "Against thee, thee only, have I sinned, and done this evil in thy sight" (Psalm 51:4, KJV).

When you compromise, you bring the world's standards into your own personal life and the church community as well.

5. Have I defined for myself the acceptable riches for my life? What do I deem important and how have I planned to achieve the goals that I have set?

Do not wear yourself out to get rich; have the wisdom to show restraint. Cast but a glance at riches, and they are gone, for they will surely sprout wings and fly off to the sky like an eagle (Prov. 23:4,5).

It is vital that the single believer makes this verse a reality in his life:

It is through these that He has given us His precious and glorious promises, so that through them, after you have escaped from the corruption that is in the world because of evil desires, you may come to share in the divine nature (2 Peter 1:4, Williams New Testament).

Decisions must be made based on priorities that favor God, not the pleasures and desires of a life that negates God and His will.

Keeping Good Company

Once you have your attitude on a positive track, you need to concentrate on developing right relationships with people. Ask yourself these questions:

1. Will I continually separate myself from the opinions of popular voices of this world in favor of what God has said?

Blessed is the man who does not walk in the counsel of the wicked or stand in the way of sinners or sit in the seat of mockers (Psalm 1:1).

Some singles worry that others will discover that they are naive about certain things. You must gain strength to resist pressure from peers, parents, and others. This means abandoning pride and fear of what others might think. You must also resist the internal pressure that says you might appear foolish in other's eyes.

Do not set foot on the path of the wicked or walk in the way of evil men (Prov. 4:14).

You must never leave the fellowship and protection of the church and go back into the world. Develop close ties to the leadership where you have been planted by the Lord. Avoid conversation and activities that will place you in opposition to what you have been taught from the Word.

2. How well do I know those around me? Are they aware of their shortcomings and working on overcoming them?

Do not make friends with a hot-tempered man, do not associate with one easily angered, or you may learn his ways and get yourself ensnared (Prov. 22:24,25).

Birds of a feather flock together. If their bad qualities rub off on you, you will find yourself shunned and labeled as an angry person that others need to avoid. You will also find yourself surrounded by angry people and entangled by deep roots of bitterness that are difficult to destroy.

Many singles experience a self-fulfilling prophecy at this time. For example, a single who is discontent with his life appears to be angry with both God and others who appear to have an "ideal" life. This anger often manifests itself in contempt for those who are happy.

The hole gets deeper, and the darkness gets more intense. Finally, the one thing that the person was believing for, the way out of loneliness, seems further from reach because of their nasty disposition.

3. Am I looking at what the ungodly have accomplished in their lives? Am I consumed with thoughts of getting ahead and not with developing godly traits in my life?

Do not envy wicked men, do not desire their company (Prov. 24:1).

You must not compare yourself with others who are not in the kingdom of God, especially in terms of why they seem to find a mate, marry, and have a family.

You must understand that God will supply your needs "according to his glorious riches in Christ Jesus" (Phil. 4:19). Don't frustrate yourself by asking, "Why do the wicked prosper?"

Endless questioning will lead you down a road that you think points toward prosperity or satisfaction when it only leads to destruction.

4. Am I exposing myself to people with proven wisdom in their lives?

He who walks with the wise grows wise, but a companion of fools suffers harm (Prov. 13:20).

Therefore do not be partners with them (Eph. 5:7).

Recognize that the unwise (fools) are headed in one direction, while the wise are headed in another. You cannot go both ways and arrive at the right destination at the proper time. Make wise decisions in every area of your life and remove the "gray areas."

The Pathway to Success

Now let's examine "the light unto our path." These guideposts or street signs, if followed, will lead you to honor.

Joseph, the son of Jacob, rose in power from slave to ruler of Egypt. He was known for his personal integrity and spiritual sensitivity. Demonstrating the wisdom of God, Joseph prepared the nation to survive a famine. All who met Joseph were aware that everywhere he went and in whatever he did, God was with him.

Joseph traveled a character-building road lit by the guideposts of God. His experiences teach us that God's presence will shed new light on dark situations. Joseph's character stands as a guidepost for all those who are striving for excellence in God. To determine if you are following Joseph's pathway, answer the questions provided.

1. Godly Influence

Spending time with God transforms every aspect of our lives. He imparts to us godly character that touches everything we do.

The Lord was with Joseph and he prospered, and he lived in the house of his Egyptian master. When his master saw that the Lord was with him and that the Lord gave him success in everything he did, Joseph found favor in his eyes . . . (Gen. 39:2-4a).

How do you compare with Joseph? Ask yourself:

• Am I seeking success without the presence of God?

• Do I have the assurance that God is with me in every situation?

• Do others see the reality of God with me?

• Have I asked for and received the favor of God for my life?

2. Good Work Ethic

A person who works to make others successful will eventually find his own success. Joseph blessed those whom he served and earned their trust.

> From the time he put him in charge of his household and of all that he owned, the Lord blessed the household of the Egyptian because of Joseph. The blessing of the Lord was on everything Potiphar had, both in the house and in the field. So he left in Joseph's care everything he had; with Joseph in charge, he did not concern himself with anything except the food he ate (Gen. 39:5,6).

How about you? Test yourself:

• Am I an example to others on my job?

• Does my supervisor need to check up on me after giving me an assignment?

3. Integrity

Your character will be tested — often when you least expect it. When faced with an opportunity to do evil, Joseph remembered that God saw his thoughts, motives, and deeds. Knowing he would eventually give an account, Joseph found the strength to resist temptation.

And after a while his master's wife took notice of Joseph and said, "Come to bed with me!" But he refused. "With me in charge," he told her, "my master does not concern himself with anything in the house; everything he owns he has entrusted to my care. No one is greater in this house than I am. My master has withheld nothing from me except you, because you are his wife. How then could I do such a wicked thing and sin against God?" (Gen. 39:7-9).

How would you answer these questions:

• Have I decided to avoid evil, whatever the cost?

• If my decisions anger others, am I willing to suffer the loss of my position?

4. God's Favor

Even in adverse circumstances, Joseph prospered. It doesn't matter what is going on around you. If you have a heart bent toward pleasing Him, God will show Himself strong on your behalf.

The Lord was with him; he showed him kindness and granted him favor in the eyes of the prison warden (Gen. 39:21).

Determine your own level of spiritual growth:

• Can others see God's hand upon my life?

• What steps have I taken to ensure that God's power is active in me and in what I do?

5. Humility

Joseph looked beyond his own adversity to the plight of his fellow prisoners. Considering their needs above his own, Joseph prepared the cupbearer and the baker for what would soon take place in their lives. His willingness to serve others eventually led to his release.

Each of the two men — the cupbearer and the baker of the king of Egypt, who were being held in prison — had a dream the same night, and each dream had a meaning of its own. When Joseph came to them the next morning, he saw that they were dejected. So he asked Pharaoh's officials who were in custody with him in his master's house, "Why are your faces so sad today?" "We both had dreams," they answered, "but there is no one to interpret them." Then Joseph said to them, "Do not interpretations belong to God? Tell me your dreams" (Gen. 40:5-8).

• Are you willing to assist others even when you are in bondage to certain unfavorable situations in your own life?

• Have you considered the cost of being forgotten by those you help out of their adversity?

6. Dependence on God

When the king was troubled by two perplexing dreams, Joseph didn't brag about his ability to give an interpretation. Instead, he pointed to God as the source of all wisdom.

Pharaoh said to Joseph, "I had a dream, and no one can interpret it. But I have heard it said of you that when you hear a dream you can interpret it." "I cannot do it," Joseph replied to Pharaoh, "but God will give Pharaoh the answer he desires" (Gen. 41:15,16).

• Are you prepared to honor God and give Him all the glory?

• Are you willing to acknowledge that without Him you can do nothing?

• When people compliment your successes, are you willing to give the credit to God?

• Are you leading people to the same source of your success?

7. Godly Boldness

Knowing what to say is one thing. Actually speaking the truth, however, often requires great boldness. Undaunted by his audience with the king, Joseph boldly declared what God had shown him.

Then Joseph said to Pharaoh, "The dreams of Pharaoh are one and the same. God has revealed to Pharaoh what he is about to do. The seven good cows are seven years, and the seven good heads of grain are seven years; it is one and the same dream. The seven lean, ugly cows that came up afterward are seven years, and so are the seven worthless heads of grain scorched by the east wind: They are seven years of famine" (Gen. 41:25-27).

• Are you bold to declare what God has given you?

8. Creativity

Merely knowing about the upcoming famine wasn't enough. The king also needed a plan to prepare his nation to endure this hardship. Joseph offered a workable solution to provide grain during the lean years that would follow the seven years of abundance.

It is just as I said to Pharaoh: God has shown Pharaoh what he is about to do. Seven years of great abundance are coming throughout the land of Egypt, but seven years of famine will follow them. Then all the abundance in Egypt will be forgotten, and the famine will ravage the land. The abundance in the land will not be remembered, because the famine that follows it will be so severe. The reason the dream was given to Pharaoh in two forms is that the matter has been firmly decided by God, and God will do it soon.

And now let Pharaoh look for a discerning and wise man and put him in charge of the land of Egypt. Let Pharaoh appoint commissioners over the land to take a fifth of the harvest of Egypt during the seven years of abundance. They should collect all the food of these good years that are coming and store up the grain under the authority of Pharaoh, to be kept in the cities for food. This food should be held in reserve for the country, to be used during the seven years of famine that will come upon Egypt, so that the country may not be ruined by the famine (Gen. 41:28-36).

• Are you willing to make innovative recommendations on the job and/or in your church without insisting that you be the one to implement them?

• Are you a team player, or do you like to "go it alone"?

• Have you demonstrated an interest in your neighbor, your community, your church, and your nation?

• What practical ways are you addressing these concerns?

The Plan Maker

The road to excellence represents your quest to become a man or woman of godly character. Becoming conformed into the image of God's Son is more important than your pursuit of earthly honors and rewards. Remember, as you delight yourself in Him, He will give you the desires of your heart.

The search for who you are must begin with who you have been destined to be in Christ!

It is because of him that you are in Christ Jesus, who has become for us wisdom from God — that is, our righteousness, holiness and redemption (1 Cor. 1:30).

In making decisions and setting goals, we cannot plan without Christ and succeed. He must not be relegated to be in our plans — He must be our plans.

But we have this treasure in jars of clay to show that this all-surpassing power is from God and not from us (2 Cor. 4:7).

The apostle Paul, a brilliant scholar, could have overwhelmed his listeners with intellectual arguments and persuasive oratory, but he shared the simple message of Jesus Christ, allowing the Holy Spirit to guide his words. He gives the reason for this in his first letter to the Corinthian Church.

My message and my preaching were not with wise and persuasive words, but with a demonstration of the Spirit's power, so that your faith might not rest on men's wisdom, but on God's power (1 Cor. 2:4,5).

Why not exercise his impressive skills? As a believer you carry far more weight than anything the world can offer you. You are the righteousness of God in Christ.

Celebrate excellence unto the Lord by giving your whole being to Him in worship and thanksgiving.

Chapter 4

You — One of a Kind!

God is unique! Scripture reveals to us only one God, but in the unity of the Godhead, three eternal, distinct, and co-equal Persons Who are the same in substance exist.

The vastness of our God is unfathomable. He is beyond human comprehension. Yet, He created us in His image and after His likeness. He blessed us and gave us the gift of His presence, which makes each of us unique.

Since God created you in His own image, this makes you unique, one of many — and, in many ways, only one. There is only one of you. People may be reminded of you through observing others, but you're one of a kind! In fact, you are so unique that God deserves from you a celebration of uniqueness. You should throw a party celebrating that He created all human beings but made you unique from all the rest.

We marvel at the uniqueness of nature. No two snowflakes are alike. We stand in awe of the complexity of the universe. God set the stars, suns, and moon in their places. But how about your uniqueness?

The psalmist describes how much God values each individual person:

> For You did form my inward parts,
> You did knit me together in my mother's womb.
> I will confess and praise You,
> For You are fearful and wonderful
> And for the awful wonder of my birth!
> Wonderful are Your works....
> My frame was not hidden from You,
> When I was being formed in secret
> And intricately and curiously wrought
> (As if embroidered with various colours)....
> Your eyes saw my unformed substance....
> How precious and weighty also are Your thoughts to me....
> If I could count them,
> They are more in number than the sand (Psalm 139:13-18, Amplified).

Even though you are fearfully and wonderfully made, you must accept yourself in Christ with all the unique attributes you possess. Can you recall when your very existence first left you in awe? Do you remember marveling at the intricacies of the human body?

When you begin to praise God for His wonderful act of love in your creation, you realize that you possess qualities of His love and life that are worth sharing with another. It is impossible to give away that love and life, however, until you first take possession of it yourself.

Many married couples have discovered this fact too late. They are bound to someone who has failed to discover and appreciate his or her own uniqueness. Because that person cannot possess his own uniqueness, he or she has difficulty accepting the uniqueness of a marriage partner.

Appreciate Your Uniqueness

God invites you to accept yourself in Christ. Once you have begun to walk in the newness of life in Christ, your self-image and self-esteem will be different than it was before.

For [as far as this world is concerned] you have died, and your [new, real] life is hid with Christ in God (Col. 3:3, Amplified).

You are no longer the person God saved. On the very day of your salvation, He began changing you from glory to glory.

You can now assert self-sufficiency in a very unique manner. The apostle Paul says that we are "self-sufficient in Christ's sufficiency" (Phil. 4:13, Amplified). He explained how we are empowered by Christ — "ready for anything and equal to anything" through Christ who infuses inner strength within us.

We live in a time of escapism. Our society encourages us not to face the pressures of life. Television, pills, and alcohol assist people in dropping out. "Stop the world, and let me off!" is the cry of many today, especially those who struggle with poor self-image. You, however, must not allow a poor self-image to rob you of the opportunity to become all that God's Word says you can be.

Therefore, if anyone is in Christ, he is a new creation; the old has gone, the new has come!... God made him who had no sin to be sin for us, so that in him we might become the righteousness of God (2 Cor. 5:17,21).

When I believed and embraced the truth of this verse, it literally changed me from a person of poor self-worth to a person who appreciates my uniqueness in Christ. Even as a youngster, I never accepted the me that God had made. I was never excited about my own personality, intellect, or sense of humor. I constantly attempted to change myself into someone I thought others would accept.

In the beginning of my ministry, evidence of this struggle emerged. Once I accepted these principles, however, I found a release in the fact that I am a "new creation" and the righteousness of God in Christ.

You, too, can experience this release as you realize the power of Scripture. You can enjoy the power of a new life in Christ.

An Internal Change

People have often thought that losing weight, getting a new hair style, or making other external changes would make them acceptable. You are already accepted in Christ. As a result of this acceptance, you have been made worthy to partake of His divine nature and enjoy the benefits of a new life.

External changes and pseudo-spiritual methodologies never take the place of hearing the Word of God, accepting it in your heart, and speaking it out of your mouth. Scripture exhorts us to be "doers of the word, and not hearers only" (James 1:22, KJV). Those who listen to the Word without acting on it only deceive themselves.

How can you get the Word of God out of your head and into your heart? You need to receive the Word with a heart inclined toward obedience and take seriously the following verse of Scripture:

And in your hearts you believe that God raised Him from the dead.... For in their hearts people exercise the faith that leads to right standing, and with their lips they make the acknowledgement which means salvation (Romans 10:9,10, Williams New Testament).

If you diligently do this, you will not yield to the temptation to compare yourself with others. Comparing your looks, your personal devotion to God, or your manner of praying only leads to more problems. If you don't succumb to feelings of inferiority, you will probably be puffed up with pride. This only makes a bad problem worse.

We do not dare to classify or compare ourselves with some who commend themselves. When they measure themselves by themselves and compare themselves with themselves, they are not wise (2 Cor. 10:12).

Learn to admire and esteem others. Follow their godly examples but never attempt to become someone that you are not.

Growth Takes Time

Learn how to properly measure your progress. Be honest with yourself but be fair!

When teaching about Christian living, I often ask, "How old are you?" I get a variety of responses from my class. A 25-year-old student looked puzzled when I asked him, "How long did it take you to get to be 25?" It's not a trick question. Obviously, it took him 25 years. Then why do we try to rush spiritual growth?

Principles involving spiritual growth may vary from those of natural growth, but one is similar to the other in terms of time. In fact, I believe one of the reasons trees are so frequently used as illustrations in Scripture is because of the time it takes for them to bear fruit. Some trees take seven years and more to produce fruit from the time of planting. We are referred to as trees of righteousness, "the branch of [his] planting . . . that [he] may be glorified" (Isaiah 60:21, KJV).

Evaluate yourself in relationship to other events that are happening in your life. Do others shift blame onto you for shortcomings in their own lives? You must learn to quickly recognize this and remove the false guilt that it brings.

You are unique to God, and your growth and development are personal to Him. Measure yourself against Christ, never others. As you behold Him, you will be changed into His image and likeness.

We Need Each Other

God desires for us to become interdependent. Our growth, if it is directed, will include becoming more of a team member than an individual player. The beauty of uniqueness is that it fits within the framework of Christ's Body and still remains outstanding.

Independence emphasizes the individual; interdependence focuses on a team or group. As a believer, you should strive for interdependence.

One young man told me he loved being by himself because he grew up in a large family. It's not unusual for young, unmarried people to feel this way if they came from such a background. A large family gives its members very little time or space to themselves. When the children grow up and live on their own, they sometimes find it a real challenge to join others in church sponsored socials, picnics, etc.

Some singles are in love with their solitude and find it difficult to be a part of a group. Yet, they are believing God for a marriage partner with whom they must share their lives — and their space!

The singles in the church I pastored for several years once brought a problem to my attention. A popular Bible teacher in the community emphasized holiness and righteousness in her teachings. While these are two essentials for a successful life in Christ, they cannot be taught as works of the flesh. They are spiritual principles and must be maintained in the context of the Spirit. If we neglect this factor in our teaching, we present an unbalanced concept of the Word of God.

The singles in our church embraced both the Word she taught and the spirit of legalism that was the fruit of her teaching emphasis. This Bible teacher's message against sexual involvement had been so strong that even in marriage many felt guilty being intimate with their mates. As a result, our ministerial staff noticed that each couple we counseled for marriage had to be deprogrammed for interdependence. Young women admitted that even though they were preparing for marriage, they found it difficult to think of giving themselves to their husbands.

Churches must be alert to bring an interdependence to their single population, rather than encouraging each of them to find their own isolated corner.

A closer tie needs to develop between the leadership of the church and the singles population. If left to themselves, singles can form independent festering pockets.

When I began to give more attention to our singles, they provided the impetus for some of our most successful discipleship efforts because they were quick to catch and foster the vision of the church. Our singles made great team leaders; and, most importantly, they learned how to become part of a team.

The Single Advantage

When singles recognize and exercise their unique capability to commit all their time, energies, and talents to seeking the kingdom of God, I believe the church will experience great revivals and moves of God. The apostle Paul indicated he had no desire to restrict the unmarried. In that same spirit of liberty regarding our single brothers and sisters, I contend that the unmarried population should be the resource for winning the world to Christ. The married population should help care for the sheep that come into the fold.

Let's contrast the concerns of the married and single believer.

I would like you to be free from concern. An unmarried man is concerned about the Lord's affairs — how he can please the Lord. But a married man is concerned about the affairs of this world — how he can please his wife — and his interests are divided.

An unmarried woman or virgin is concerned about the Lord's affairs: Her aim is to be devoted to the Lord in both body and spirit. But a married woman is concerned about the affairs of this world — how she can please her husband. I am saying this for your own good, not to restrict you, but that you may live in a right way in undivided devotion to the Lord (1 Cor. 7:32-35).

How you see yourself in your singleness is a matter of selective perception. It involves looking at the good things, rather than frustrating yourself over what you don't have. Evaluate your perception of what marriage might bring into your life. Is it security? Is it a new car or a new home? Do you perceive your prosperity to be wrapped up in marriage?

Although God does promise prosperity for His children, we must remember that we are not in this world to own a house. We are not here to own a car or to have a good job. We are here to glorify God — to show the world there is a God who rules and reigns with power and majesty.

As we glorify God in our lives, He will prosper us. Our very prosperity is a testimony and a celebration unto the Lord. Banish the thought that you are here merely to work, to buy clothes, or to get a husband or a wife. God understands exactly what you need, and He knows the desires of your heart. Believe me, prosperity is not obtained through marriage, but by God and God alone.

That's why Scripture tells us to "seek first his kingdom and his righteousness, and all these things will be given to you as well" (Matt. 6:33). The kingdom of God is His first concern. God will give you a good house or a nice car as a testimony of His Lordship. It just looks better for His children to be well cared for.

Can you see the distinct advantage the single person has to seek first the kingdom of God? You have the opportunity to serve God totally, caring for the things of His kingdom without regard to daily pressures from others, such as a husband or wife.

When you marry, your affections change. It is ungodly for a married man to care totally for the things of God, ignoring the needs of his family. Paul warned that the married man will naturally care for the things of this world, how he might please his wife.

Paul repeated this theme: "Whoever fails to provide for his own relatives, and especially for those in this immediate family, has disowned the faith and is worse than an unbeliever" (1 Tim. 5:8, Williams New Testament).

Pursuing Oneness

There is a difference between "one" and "single" in God's eyes. There is also a difference between "one" and "unmarried." God said two shall become one. Two people with individual personalities join to become one in marriage. The two struggle to become one at home; when they get to church, they struggle to be one with the church.

While you are single, you can recognize the struggles that married couples face. Learn now to adjust to others so whenever you marry, bonding can take place easier and more quickly. Bless the Lord and celebrate your singleness! For now, you need only concern yourself with being one with the Body of Christ.

This is not an insult to singles. Rather, the godly, kingdom principle of being joined to the body can be exercised early in your life as a single rather than waiting until you have joined another in marriage.

Jesus Himself prayed for this unity: "That they all may be one; as thou, Father, art in me, and I in thee, that they also may be one in us:

that the world may believe that thou hast sent me" (John 17:21, KJV). When singles purpose in their hearts to pursue this prayer at any cost, they seek the kingdom of God.

Begin to look at your singleness as a blessing. Start praising the Lord and thanking Him that you have this time alone!

God is not punishing you with singleness. You have not been plagued with a disease. God doesn't need the help of a mate to conform you to His image. You are the beloved of the Lord. When you uncompromisingly accept His standards as your own, you communicate to God and affirm in your own heart that all of His judgments are righteous altogether.

Many singles struggle with restrictions on whom they should relate to. If God says to restrict your intimate relationships to people who are believers, accept this as a unique feature of His love for you. Never compromise His principles to meet your physical or emotional needs. Rather than making the life-long mistake of being unequally yoked, the single's eyes should be upon the Lord.

Many singles, like King Jehoshaphat, face overwhelming odds. When several armies threatened to attack Judah, the king's troops were outnumbered. The possibility of survival looked bleak, but Jehoshaphat prayed: ". . . neither know we what to do: but our eyes are upon thee" (2 Chron. 20:12, KJV).

In keeping their eyes on the Lord, singles uphold the standards of the Word, and God is glorified in everything that occurs in their lives.

"Let the wicked forsake his way, and the unrighteous man his thoughts.... For my thoughts are not your thoughts, neither are your ways my ways" (Isaiah 55:7,8, KJV).

Even after you are forgiven, you must make the thoughts and ways of the Lord your own. Search the Scriptures for the many times

God instructs us to renew our minds. After extolling the virtues of wholesome thoughts, He tells us to "think about such things" (Phil. 4:8) and "let the peace of Christ rule in your hearts" (Col. 3:15).

God wants to make your thoughts His. Reflect upon the fact that His thoughts of you outnumber the grains of sand. Indeed you are unique unto God.

Specially Selected

Understand your special selection and lean on it for your acceptance, security, and self-image. There are no more important elements than these three things in a person's life.

When you opt for worldly acceptance, you cast yourself into the chaos of constantly changing rules. You find yourself patterning your life after what will get you accepted by a certain crowd at a certain time. But one mistake is to keep abreast with the "in crowd," and you're out!

Your special selection is enfolded in God's love for you. Nothing can be added or taken away from it. He loved you while you were an enemy and accepted you into His kingdom while you were a stranger. You can't add to that.

"He hath made us accepted in the beloved" (Eph. 1:6, KJV). As Christ paid the price for your sins, He also became the means of God's acceptance. God views you as a gift. "Moreover, because of what Christ has done we have become gifts to God that he delights in" (Eph. 1:11, TLB).

Your special selection makes you a gift. When youngsters are given gifts, they radiate with joy. They glow with excitement at having received something special. That same joy must be allowed to flow through us as adults when we recognize that we are gifts of God!

God actually delights in us as gifts to Himself through Christ. He rejoices and is exuberant to receive us. When you feel your life has little value, you can draw on His acceptance for joy.

Through Him (Christ) He picked us out before the creation of the world . . . He foreordained us to become His sons . . . to carry out the happy choice of His will (Eph. 1:4,5, Williams New Testament).

You have been specially selected — hand-picked by God for Himself. Failing to focus on this can breed depression at times. The results of depression are devastating if you see yourself as a person of little or no worth.

What are you measuring your value against? Are you plagued with the following thoughts: Who would ever want me? I'm too old! I'm not worthy to be loved. You must realize that God never ages and that His promises are good forever.

Finding satisfaction "in Christ" and being fulfilled with Him needs to express itself in a spiritual rather than a physical sense. Because we are flesh and blood, spiritual satisfaction breeds a godly physical satisfaction, which results in security. This sense of safety and peace is incomprehensible in human terms and comes as a result of understanding your special selection.

Secure in Christ

When you are feeling insecure, focus on the words of Jesus to His disciples:

Do not let your hearts be troubled. Trust in God; trust also in me. In my Father's house are many rooms; if it were not so, I would have told you. I am going there to prepare a place for you. And if I go and prepare a place for you, I will come back and take you to be with me that you also may be where I am. You know the way to the place where I am going (John 14:1-4).

In my many discussions with singles, I've seen several recurring emotions. They feel alone, abandoned, forsaken with little sense of security in their lives. Unable to see God's purposes, they find it difficult to focus on their uniqueness.

Jesus' promised return gave His disciples a sense of security. That same sense of security can be evident in the single believer's life as you learn two important principles:

1. The first object of your affection should not be toward another human being. Most believers invest very little preparation into being single. Most of us were trained to prepare for marriage; thus, our focus became finding the right person upon whom we could lavish our affection.

On the other hand, if you have been trained to be secure in the love of God, to accept where you are and rejoice in His provisions, you will give Him praise. You will celebrate!

> According as he hath chosen us in him before the foundation of the world, that we should be holy and without blame before him in love (Eph. 1:4, KJV).

This is the foundation for special selection. God chose you. You did not choose Him.

Your focus determines your success or failure in life. Adjusting your focus toward God transforms discouragement to great courage and fear into faith!

2. Failing to focus on the promises of God will wither your hope. When we fail to focus on God's Word, our hope has no feeding place. "Let us fix our eyes on Jesus.... Consider Him . . . so that you will not grow weary and lose heart" (Hebrews 12:2,3).

Granted, this sounds simple. You undoubtedly wonder if you can read a book or talk to someone who understands what it's really like to be single. This admonition, however, was aimed at satisfying the requirements of both married and single believers. Fix your eyes on Jesus.

I got into my wife's car one day and headed down the hill away from our home. Since she drives the car most of the time, the rearview mirror was positioned for her vision. I didn't take the time to readjust it. When I reached the bottom of the hill and entered the flow of traffic, I looked in the mirror for direction. My image glared back at me, blocking the traffic behind me from view.

Distracted by my inability to see behind me, I found myself swerving to miss an oncoming vehicle. Because of the unnatural focus on the mirror (seeing only my face), I had lost focus on what was before me — and control of my vehicle. Why? Because my eyes were fixed on me. My countenance filled the entire rearview mirror.

We can, without fully realizing it, block the future and obscure the past when we focus on ourselves or others, resulting in an inaccurate perspective of our present circumstances.

What You Really Need

Today holds limitless possibilities. We will never experience them, however, if we're chained to the past. Peter and John met a man who could have let his past prevent him from being healed in a miraculous way.

Now a man crippled from birth was being carried to the temple gate called Beautiful, where he was put every day to beg from those going into the temple courts. When he saw Peter and John about to enter, he asked them for money.

Peter looked straight at him, as did John. Then Peter said, "Look at us!" So the man gave them his attention, expecting to get something from them. Then Peter said, "Silver or gold I do not have, but what I have I give you. In the name of Jesus Christ of Nazareth, walk."

Taking him by the right hand, he helped him up, and instantly the man's feet and ankles became strong. He jumped to his feet and began to walk. Then he went with them into the temple courts, walking and jumping, and praising God (Acts 3:2-8).

The crippled man looked for the help of others to sustain him in his misery, but what he really needed was health for his body and soul. This man needed to ponder the question of the psalmist and heed his conclusion: "I lift up my eyes to the hills — where does my help come from? My help comes from the Lord, the Maker of heaven and earth" (Psalm 121:1,2).

Crippled from birth and with no hope for the future, this man could have let his past circumstances keep him bound. Fortunately for him, Peter redirected his focus to the name of Jesus Christ of Nazareth!

When a person uses relationships, or the hope of a future relationship, to feel secure in who he or she is, there is only trouble ahead. A man may look to a woman, giving her attention and expecting to receive something from her in return. When he doesn't receive what he's looking for, he suffers tremendous hurt and a sagging self-image. He begins to measure his importance by the very standards by which he was rejected.

As illustrated by the account of the crippled man in the Book of Acts, what we think we want and what we actually need are totally incompatible.

You must keep your eyes on Jesus, not on trying to find ways to eliminate the circumstances of your singleness. Your security is in Jesus. It is not in your ability, good looks, or lack of good looks. It is not in whether you are single or married.

Selective Perception

Don't underestimate the importance of a positive self-image. On the other hand, don't over-emphasize the importance of a positive self-image. Sound contradictory? It isn't really. It is matter of having a sober opinion of your own importance.

Your self-image cannot be left to other people. Find out what God's Word says about you. Determine to think of yourself in that way. Again, exercise selective perception.

Let me show you the secret of a positive self-image, self-acceptance, and self-worth.

. . . set your minds and keep them set on what is above — the higher things — not on the things that are on the earth. For [as far as this world is concerned] you have died, and your [new, real] life is hid with Christ in God (Col. 3:2,3, Amplified).

What a sobering thought. I died! The old nature that Satan tries to resurrect is dead. I loved him once, but I am now eternally separated from the old man. He died, and my new life is hidden in Christ.

No negative elements can penetrate the protective wall that is with Christ in God. As you resign from living according to the world's standards, you can enjoy God's power in your life.

Many of us have experienced the death of people very dear to us. Somehow the healing power of God's Word works in us an exceeding weight of glory that brings comfort and a sense that all is well. As you let them go, you mature.

You must follow the same process when it comes to letting the old man die. You must mature, let go, and accept the new creature status that God paid for in Christ.

If then you have died with Christ to material ways of looking at things and have escaped from the world's crude and elemental notions and teachings of externalism, why do you live as if you still belong to the world? — Why do you submit to rules and regulations? (Col. 2:20, Amplified).

When you decide to celebrate unto the Lord, think of His goodness to kill your old self and resurrect you in Him — in a new image conformed to God in both character and principle.

A single woman told me that her greatest fear was that God did not share her deepest concerns. God seemed not to care about her getting older and not being married. He did not seem to be concerned that she had grown weary of being alone.

Only God would have the patience to stay with us during these times. Only God would be long-suffering enough to listen and not judge us when we feel alone.

In our human experience we need to know that God is able to provide for us. Many feel that since God is Spirit, they still need a man or woman that they can feel, touch, hear, and be heard by. Our Maker poses this question: "Am I a God at hand . . . and not a God afar off?" (Jer. 23:23, KJV).

No matter what challenges you face, God is not punishing you with singleness. God accepts you unconditionally and loves you passionately. When you accept that fact, you can be secure in Him and enjoy a positive self-image. You can celebrate your uniqueness before the Lord!

Chapter 5

God's Framework for Relationships

Everyone loves peaceful, harmonious relationships. But what undergirds a friendship or marriage to keep it from being destroyed by conflict and discord? Order defines the framework in which relationships thrive.

Order denotes a harmonious relationship between two or more elements or persons; it's a logical sequence or rank. The order of God encompasses every part of this definition. When we insist on doing things our own way, we miss God's order.

God has a prescribed order for reaching adulthood and maturity. Most teenagers, however, would like to discard it when they get to that developmental stage of life.

Even secular pursuits, such as an education or a career, demand a certain progression in order to reach certain goals. Many of us would like to skip some of the tedious processes. When we try to opt out of prescribed steps, however, we usually find that each learning step was necessary to accomplishing our goals.

Edmund Burke once stated, "Good order is the foundation of all good things." If there is to be good in terms of singles finding their place in the scheme of relationships and life objectives, good order must be established and maintained.

Let's discuss three elements that, when activated, form the basis of order in the single's life.

1. Set realistic goals.

2. Develop your character.

3. Rely on God's promises.

Be Realistic!

One evening I invited a group of singles to my home and asked them what they thought were some unrealistic goals for singles. Here are some of the answers:

"I want to be married by my thirtieth birthday."

"I want to purchase and completely furnish my home before I get married."

"I want to make a lot of money so I won't be financially dependent on anyone when I get married."

What is so unrealistic about these goals? Because you control only your own will, you can't guarantee marriage by a certain age. Your goals shouldn't eliminate a daily dependence on God or set prerequisites to His work in your life. God encourages us with these words, "For I know the plans I have for you . . . plans to prosper you and not to harm you, plans to give you hope and a future" (Jer. 29:11).

You cannot return from a trip that you did not take. You need a plan! You need to know what you propose to accomplish in your life and how you believe God will bring it about.

Without a plan you will always be frustrated. You are dependent on outside circumstances to line up and become favorable before you will take action. With set goals and a plan to accomplish those goals, your direction will be clear, and you will have a fuller life of peace and joy.

A goal is defined as the end or ultimate purpose toward which an endeavor is directed. Of course, our ultimate goal is to be like Jesus.

Dear friends, now we are children of God, and what we will be has not yet been made known. But we know that when he appears, we shall be like him, for we shall see him as he is (1 John 3:2).

In the meantime, what are the steps to be taken to be like Him? What plans do you have to make your time on this earth meaningful, rich, and fulfilling?

Everyone who has this hope in him purifies himself, just as he is pure (1 John 3:3).

Set goals for developing the kind of character that will bring joy to someone else's life. If God's plan is for you to marry, you will be a blessing to your spouse. Incorporate objectives in your career goals (school teacher, chemist, etc.) that will glorify God beyond just achieving the position. Work on having a godly attitude and a persevering spirit.

Identify negative patterns in your family life and work at correcting or eliminating them. Institute new patterns that will enhance your life and your family's life.

One day I met with a single minister friend. He was wrestling with some decisions in his life and wanted me to pray with him. This gifted young man, successful by worldly standards, was feeling very empty and confused. He knew he basically lacked character. Projecting a public image that differed from his private life, he was not very pleased with the gap and had actually contemplated suicide.

"Why do you want to take your life?" I asked him.

"Because I don't like the lie I am projecting to others," he replied.

This crisis led him to discover a very important principle: Being honest with yourself is a life saver.

After we talked and prayed together, he decided to remove himself from an unhealthy spiritual environment and submit himself to a ministry that stressed a godly standard for the development of character. His decision resulted in a well-rounded, much happier young man who now has his life in order.

Jesus is the only mark worth aiming for. We must learn to set our sights on Christ, making Him the object of all our considerations.

And my preaching was very plain, not with a lot of oratory and human wisdom, but the Holy Spirit's power was in my words, proving to those who heard them that the message was from God. I did this because I wanted your faith to stand firmly upon God, not on man's great ideas (1 Cor. 2:4,5, TLB).

The key to successful goal-setting is to narrow your options. You are a believer, not a doubter. You believe the Word of God and do not distrust what it says to you. Narrow your options to the Word of God, and you will be able to succeed with the goals you set.

A golf player in a U.S. Open, after hitting a shot down the fairway, was complimented by a bystander. "Good shot," said the bystander. With respect, but determination, the professional golfer turned to the bystander and said, "I see that we live by different standards in golf."

Celebrate God's order in your life. Recognize who He is and who you are. "The Lord is God.... We are his people, the sheep of his pasture" (Psalm 100:3).

Meeting the Prerequisites

Are you convinced that God loves you more than you love yourself and that He is more concerned about your welfare than you are? To answer that question, let's examine the biblical account of Isaac and Rebekah.

Abraham, by then an old man, expressed concerned about finding a wife for his son, Isaac. When he sent for his faithful servant, Eliezer, Abraham made him swear not to take a wife for Isaac from the nations around them but to go back to his own country to find the wife God had chosen for his son.

The servant swore an oath and prepared to carry out Abraham's orders. During his journey, Eliezer prayed, "O Lord, God of my master Abraham, give me success today" (Gen. 24:12).

Our prayer lives must be filled with God's desires. God wants us to prosper and have good success. As a single person, don't waste your time looking for some person who can make you happy. Instead, spend your time asking God to make your way prosperous and successful.

Eliezer's prayer for success was answered quickly. He met Rebekah, who invited him to spend the night with her family. Refusing to eat until he had shared the purpose for his journey, Eliezer explained the providential circumstances that led him there.

My master made me swear an oath, and said, "You must not get a wife for my son from the daughters of the Canaanites, in whose land I live, but go to my father's family and to my own clan, and get a wife for my son." Then I asked my master,

"What if the woman will not come back with me?" He replied, "The Lord, before whom I have walked, will send his angel with you and make your journey a success.... Then, when you go to my clan, you will be released from my oath even if they refuse to give her to you . . ."

When I came to the spring today, I said, "O Lord, God of my master Abraham, if you will, please grant success to the journey on which I have come. See, I am standing beside this spring; if a maiden comes out to draw water and I say to her, "Please let me drink a little water from your jar," and if she says to me, "Drink, and I'll draw water for your camels too," let her be the one the Lord has chosen for my master's son. Before I finished praying in my heart, Rebekah came out, with her jar on her shoulder. She went down to the spring and drew water, and I said to her, "Please give me a drink." She quickly lowered her jar from her shoulder and said, "Drink, and I'll water your camels too."

. . . Laban and Bethuel answered, "This is from the Lord; we can say nothing to you one way or the other. Here is Rebekah; take her and go, and let her become the wife of your master's son, as the Lord has directed . . ." Then they said, "Let's call the girl and ask her about it." So they called Rebekah and asked her, "Will you go with this man?" "I will go," she said (Gen. 24:37-46,50,57,58).

This passage illustrates three prerequisites for success:

1. The girl must be willing to work.

2. She must possess a heart to follow.

3. Her family must be willing to release her.

The servant symbolizes the Holy Spirit as He goes to find that willing soul wanting to accept Jesus. God sends forth the Holy Spirit to find brides for His Son. His Son gladly receives all those who come to the Father by Him and refuses to turn any away.

Rebekah met the prerequisites. She represents the willing who rejoice at the opportunity to be saved from a life of misery and to enter the presence of God. She is willing to follow wherever she is asked to go. Finally, she leaves her family in order to be joined to her husband. What a tremendous testimony of God's love and our response to it.

The servant provides us with an excellent example of the character traits we should develop as we are entrusted with lives that are to be presented back to the Father.

1. He is dependable and trustworthy. "Abraham . . . said to the chief servant in his household, the one in charge of all he had . . ." (24:1,2).

2. He is a praying person. "Then he prayed, 'O Lord, God of my master Abraham, give me success today . . .'" (24:12).

3. He is so earnest that he refuses to eat before attending to his master's business. "Then food was set before him, but he said, 'I will not eat until I have told you what I have to say'" (24:33).

4. He never speaks his own name but is always speaking about his master. "I am Abraham's servant. The Lord has blessed my master abundantly, and he has become wealthy" (24:34,35).

5. He gives God all the glory. "I bowed down and worshiped the Lord. I praised the Lord, the God of my master Abraham, who had led me on the right road . . ." (24:48).

Let's make the effort to incorporate these principles into our lives as believers — single and married. Do I have the testimony of God that He is trustworthy and dependable? If so, am I trustworthy and dependable in His eyes?

Am I a person of prayer? Do I constantly seek the will of God in my actions, thoughts, and decisions? As one adage puts it: Why worry when you can pray, or why pray when you can worry? Which am I doing?

Do I really put the things of God first in my life? Is He exalted by my thoughts and actions? Can others see my love and devotion to Him? Will I put His will before my own needs?

Am I self-centered? Do I constantly speak my name and my wants, or is God's name always on my lips? Is He honored supremely in my life? Do I agree with the words of John the Baptist: "He must become greater; I must become less"? (John 3:30).

Am I determined to praise God for whatever happens in my life? Do I know that God is for me, working to bring all things to my good because I love Him? Do I truly glory in tribulation, testings, and trials? Does God get the glory from my life?

These questions must be answered before you can determine the degree to which you are fulfilling the principles in your everyday life.

Can You Trust God?

The story ends when Isaac and Rebekah see each other for the first time with the eyes of total acceptance of God's blessing. "Isaac brought her into the tent of his mother Sarah, and he married Rebekah. So she became his wife, and he loved her . . ." (Gen. 24:67).

God can be trusted with your future. You will like what God brings you. He constantly looks for your good. Are you able to trust Him to bring the right person into your life as Isaac trusted Eliezer and his father?

When we celebrate order, we celebrate the fact that tricks, schemes, and other worldly methods need not be employed in order to bring attention to ourselves. God will get us noticed. He will make sure the right person is placed in our paths.

For men, this means that the quest to love will be satisfied. A man usually searches many to love, while a woman seeks one to which she can be joined.

For the woman, this means her quest to be joined will be fulfilled in a godly manner. When God told Eve in the garden that her desire was to be to her husband, it was not a curse but a divine order being put into place.

Can I trust the work of the Holy Spirit to expose me to the people I need to know and to bring me a life partner?

If it is the will of God, can I live as a single person for the rest of my life? Before you answer this question, let's consider some biblical teaching regarding the will of God.

First, we should not make definite plans for our lives. Instead, we are to say, "If it is the Lord's will, we will live and do this or that" (James 4:15).

Please don't confuse this with teachings built upon the premise that if you know God's Word, you know God's will. It is not that simple in areas where His will is not clearly spelled out.

We must constantly subject our thoughts, expectations, hopes, dreams, and our very lives to God, understanding that His will has priority over our own wills. Your will becomes His only as you submit it to Him.

Be very careful, then, how you live — not as unwise but as wise, making the most of every opportunity, because the days are evil. Therefore do not be foolish, but understand what the Lord's will is (Eph. 5:15-17).

While traveling throughout England and Australia, I had difficulty adjusting to their traffic patterns and driving habits. While riding in a car, I fell asleep and awakened startled because I momentarily thought that I was supposed to be driving. After all, I was on the left side (the American driver's side) of the vehicle.

I stepped off a curb in Australia and was almost hit by an oncoming car because I thought the approaching traffic should be coming from my left. "Look both ways before you cross the street," my mother told me as a child. I looked left, right, and left again. Stepping into the street traffic, I was shocked when oncoming cars suddenly appeared from my right.

Sometimes we think that we understand the Word of God because we have heard it again and again. We think we know what God will do merely because we have seen Him move in previous circumstances in a similar way. None of us are acquainted with heaven's traffic patterns.

We cannot simply look left, right, and left again and step out into the street. God will surely move differently than we suppose. If we learn to submit to His will, I am convinced that we will definitely be happier, not to mention safer, people.

I have talked with many people who aspired to be married. As soon as they were willing to remain single for the rest of their days, God sent the right person into their lives.

Hebrews 10:29 says some have "insulted the spirit of grace." You insult the Spirit of Grace by not submitting to His will and counsel for your life but insisting on your own way.

Notice among yourselves, dear brothers, that few of you who follow Christ have big names or power or wealth. Instead, God has deliberately chosen to use ideas the world considers foolish and of little worth in order to shame those people considered by the world as wise and great (1 Cor. 1:26,27, TLB).

Our ideas, dreams, and hopes usually conflict with God's ideas, His dreams, and His hopes. Yielding produces a willingness in us to trust His counsel and wisdom.

All to Jesus, I surrender, all to Him I freely give.

I will ever love and trust Him, in His presence daily live.

I surrender all. I surrender all.

All to Thee my Blessed Savior, I surrender all.

The songwriter reminds us that yielding is an act of total surrender. This surrender to God, however, must be accompanied by love and trust. When we love and trust God, delighting in Him, we desire to abide with Him and He with us.

Before any yielding occurs, willingness must be present. Whenever willingness produces yielding, God's will for our lives unfolds. As mentioned before in Jeremiah 29:11, God's thoughts toward the believer are thoughts of good and not of evil, to give hope and a future.

You can now embark on a celebration of order. You have surrendered your will to Him, and He has turned your captivity into laughter and joy. Once imprisoned by your own ideas, dreams, and hopes, you are now released from the care of yourself. You are free to celebrate unto Him for all that He has done in your life — and will do in your future.

God's Guarantee

God's promises grow with people. You can never outlive a promise of God!

When God appeared to Abram and invited him to walk in faith, God said, "Leave your home, your relatives, and go to a place where

I will lead you." Abram accepted God's invitation. Because of his faith, God credited him with righteousness, naming him the father of faith.

God promised Abram that he would be the father of many nations. Many years passed, but no child came from Abram's loins. When God reaffirmed His promise to Abram (now Abraham), both he and his wife, Sarah, laughed. "Sarah, too, had faith, and because of this she was able to become a mother in spite of her old age, for she realized that God, who gave her his promise, would certainly do what he said" (Hebrews 11:11, TLB). Their exact response to the promise of God is not recorded in the New Testament, only that God was pleased with their faithfulness.

This is a source of hope for singles who have wearied in well-doing. God has placed specific and non-specific promises in His Word. The fact that He promised is a guarantee those promises will come to pass.

> God also bound himself with an oath, so that those he promised to help would be perfectly sure and never need to wonder whether he might change his plans. He has given us both his promise and his oath, two things we can completely count on, for it is impossible for God to tell a lie (Hebrews 6:17,18, TLB).

Let me take this principle to the extreme. If it is God's will for you to marry at age 97, you will have your day. You will walk down the aisle in grand style. I am not being funny. You cannot outlive the promises of God.

Perhaps the prospect of marriage at age 97 seems like a bad joke. After all, we have a lot of emotions and affections that need to be shared before a certain age. We want sexual fulfillment before we are too old to experience it or remember the pleasure.

While this is a reality, you must remember that whatever is born of God overcomes the world! We overcome the world's systems and orders. Everything will be in place. Remember God will keep His promises.

If Abraham and Sarah waited for over 20 years for the promise of a child to be fulfilled, how long are you willing to wait? Age doesn't matter. If you are to marry, you will marry.

Hoping Against Hope

Waiting for anything can be difficult. Although Abraham was married, he and his wife Sarah waited for years before God's promise regarding their son came to pass.

Singles can learn some valuable lessons from the patriarch's life. Let's look at Abraham's character between God's promise and the fulfillment of that expectation.

As it is written: "I have made you a father of many nations." He is our father in the sight of God, in whom he believed — the God who gives life to the dead and calls things that are not as though they were. Against all hope, Abraham in hope believed and so became the father of many nations, just as it had been said to him, "So shall your offspring be." Without weakening in his faith, he faced the fact that his body was as good as dead — since he was about one hundred years old — and that Sarah's womb was also dead. Yet he did not waver through unbelief regarding the promises of God, but was strengthened in his faith and gave glory to God, being fully persuaded that God had power to do what he had promised (Romans 4:17-21).

Incorporating Abraham's attitudes into the single life can turn hardship in abstaining into a celebration of celibacy unto the Lord. You can carry yourself as a gift into marriage.

Let's look at each point.

1. Abraham hoped against hope. "[For Abraham, human reason for] hope being gone, hoped on in faith" (Romans 4:18, Amplified). When all human reason for hope was gone, Abraham hoped in faith. Hope, which cannot be built on human reasoning or logic, is definitely a work of the Spirit of God. At times the single will have to position himself against hopelessness.

2. Abraham was not weak in faith when faced with circumstances. At times an individual may grow weak, but he must make sure that the weakness does not touch his faith. Weak means feeble in any sense. You must guard against being feeble in your believing, trusting, and relying on the integrity of God and His Word.

3. Abraham did not waiver in doubt and unbelief. The word "waiver" means to separate thoroughly, to withdraw from; oppose; to hesitate. Abraham did not separate himself from the promise of God. Singles must not allow doubt and unbelief to separate them from God's exceedingly great promises.

Doubt and unbelief oppose your faith in God. The word "doubt" is from the same root word "waiver," meaning to be between two points and uncertain about which one to take; to be without a way or resources. Singles need to guard against the feeling of being without a way and without resources. God will make sure that your mate, if you are to marry, is in place when the time is right.

Remember the words that Paul wrote to the believers at Corinth: "We are hard pressed on every side, but not crushed; perplexed, but not in despair; persecuted, but not abandoned; struck down, but not destroyed" (2 Cor. 4:8,9).

4. Abraham was strong in faith, giving glory to God. This implies that his strength grew instead of waning. You may feel that you can no longer keep your body and thoughts sanctified to God, but you can, like Abraham, increase in the strength of God.

How do you gain strength? Time in the Word and fellowship with stronger believers will encourage you to pursue the things of God. Don't be discouraged by progress checkered with defeat in the area of abstinence. Purity of heart, thought, and action comes in gradual steps.

5. *Abraham was "fully persuaded"* (KJV) that God would keep His promise. Strong's Concordance tells us the original language reads "most surely believed." After becoming discouraged in your singleness, gather your thoughts and say, "I most surely believe that what God said, He will do!"

This is a winning attitude! Nothing can stop the believer who adopts this mind-set from celebrating unto the Lord.

Woman For Man?

God has articulated His order in His Word so that generations to come might know what is expected of them in interpersonal relationships, especially between marriage partners. Marriage, however, is not the only goal for order regarding male/female relationships. Singles can begin now to identify with the need to allow God to give definition to this aspect of their lives, thus bringing all other elements into focus.

The Book of Proverbs says, "He who finds a wife finds what is good and receives favor from the Lord" (Prov. 18:22). The responsibility, then, for finding a mate rests on the man — not on the woman. That is God's order.

For those who have entered into engagement, these points will bear great relevance. Even single believers, however, must grasp that God's love is above all else.

"Let all things be done decently and in order" (1 Cor. 14:40, KJV).

God demands order. His Word declares that He is not the author of confusion. While the world fights over personal rights, the Word of God is clear when it comes to responsibility.

For Adam was formed first, then Eve (1 Tim. 2:13).

For man did not come from woman, but woman from man; neither was man created for woman, but woman for man (1 Cor. 11:8,9).

These verses do not speak of inferiority or superiority. They speak of order. They proclaim that in the eyes of God, He expects man to protect, cover, and love the woman. That responsibility is not contingent upon an approved response from the woman.

God's order begins to express itself in the role of men in life — not just in marriage but in all life situations. For example, if more men understood headship prior to marriage, many of the problems they encounter after marriage would never occur.

Single men and women need to understand headship before marriage. It is not something to be worked out after the wedding ceremony.

The order of God also says the man is the head of the woman. The apostle Paul wrote, "Now I want you to realize that the head of every man is Christ, and the head of the woman is man, and the head of Christ is God" (1 Cor. 11:3). "Head" does not mean that the man does all the thinking and deciding. It does not mean that the woman is incapable of making suggestions. It does mean that God holds him responsible for the level of spiritual achievement that the family makes under his leadership.

Let's look at an example of a man who refused to lead his wife and suffered dire consequences. The story of Ahab and Jezebel provides the classic example of a marriage out of order.

King Ahab desired the vineyard of Naboth. When he asked for it, Naboth refused, telling Ahab that it was an inheritance and, therefore, could not be given away. His answer grieved Ahab and left him "sullen and angry," so he lay in bed, refusing to eat.

His wife Jezebel came in and asked him, "Why are you so sullen? Why won't you eat?" He answered her, "Because . . . Naboth the Jezreelite . . . said, 'I will not give you my vineyard.'" Jezebel his wife said, "Is this how you act as king over Israel? Get up and eat! Cheer up. I'll get you the vineyard of Naboth the Jezreelite."

So she wrote letters in Ahab's name, placed his seal on them, and sent them to the elders and nobles who lived in Naboth's city with him.... So the elders and nobles who lived in Naboth's city did as Jezebel directed in the letters she had written to them. They proclaimed a fast and seated Naboth in a prominent place among the people. Then two scoundrels came and sat opposite him and brought charges against Naboth before the people, saying, "Naboth has cursed both God and the king." So they took him outside the city and stoned him to death....

As soon as Jezebel heard that Naboth had been stoned to death, she said to Ahab, "Get up and take possession of the vineyard of Naboth the Jezreelite that he refused to sell you. He is no longer alive but dead" (1 Kings 21:5-8,11-13,15).

Seeing how disheartened Ahab had become at Naboth's refusal, Jezebel devised a wicked plot to gain the vineyard for her husband. She wrote letters to the civic leaders of the kingdom in her husband's name and sealed them with the king's seal, which resulted in the death of an innocent man. Then she smugly reported to her husband the news. "You know the vineyard Naboth wouldn't sell you? Well, you can have it now! He's dead!"

Ahab gladly claimed Naboth's vineyard as his own, but he paid a huge price for satisfying his desire:

> Then the word of the Lord came to Elijah the Tishbite: "Go down to meet Ahab king of Israel, who rules in Samaria. He is now in Naboth's vineyard, where he has gone to take posses- sion of it. Say to him, 'This is what the Lord says: Have you not murdered a man and seized his property?' Then say to him, 'This is what the Lord says: In the place where the dogs licked up Naboth's blood, dogs will lick up your blood . . . I will consume your descendants and cut off from Ahab every last male in Israel — slave or free'" (1 Kings 21:17-19,21).

Although Ahab had not actually arranged the death of Naboth, God held him accountable! The Lord sent a message to Ahab by Elijah, cursing him, his wife, and all his descendants!

Restoring Hope

Many singles have lost hope. Having an accurate knowledge of order, however, will help establish the single believer's hope in the future.

"Hope deferred maketh the heart sick" (Prov. 13:12, KJV). For many singles, it is impossible for faith to spring forth from their hearts because they are "heartsick." They desperately need to come back to God's order, celebrate it, and see God bring all things to- gether for them.

To alleviate this hopelessness, two important things need to take place. First, the single must become "kingdom conscious." Second, the Church must teach a solid word that keeps singles connected to the whole Body of Christ.

To establish and maintain order, the single need only ask himself this question: "Can I trust the work of the Holy Spirit to both expose me to the people I need to know and to bring me a life partner?" It is easier to believe God for the same measure of success that Eliezer experienced when both parties are submitted to the Holy Spirit and to the leadership of their respective churches.

I am often asked by single Christians, "What if God were to give me someone that I don't particularly like? What if he's not my type?" Remember, God made both you and the person He will bring you. Why would His taste be different from yours? God gave you your taste.

The person that God will bring into your life will be the person that will grow with you, provide an inheritance with you, and excel in the things of God with you. They may be buffed, curved, cute, or not so cute, but they definitely will be "graced" to be with you.

If there is to be a celebration, it must include trust in God, faith in His Word, knowing that God is on our side, and obtaining a thorough knowledge that the Holy Spirit works within us to bring us to a place of rest and peace.

Take time to study God's order and see how He has caused life to have harmony. As you learn how to cooperate with that order, you will experience the perfection of His will in your life.

Chapter 6

Successful Single Parenting

Single heads of households face many seemingly insurmountable challenges. Out-of-wedlock pregnancies trap many young women in a cycle of poverty and dependence upon government programs. If she becomes suddenly single as a result of divorce, a woman's income usually plummets drastically. Deadbeat dads fail to pay child support, forcing their former spouse into the workforce where women still earn considerably less than men.

Even though the number of households headed by a single parent has ballooned over the past decade, their challenges are not new. The prophet Elijah met a despairing and destitute widow.

Then the Lord said to him, "Go and live in the village of Zarephath, near the city of Sidon. There is a widow there who will feed you. I have given her my instructions."

So he went to Zarephath. As he arrived at the gates of the city he saw a widow gathering sticks; and he asked her for a cup of water. As she was going to get it, he called to her, "Bring me a bite of bread, too."

But she said, "I swear by the Lord your God that I haven't a single piece of bread in the house. And I have only a handful of flour left and a little cooking oil in the bottom of the jar. I was just gathering a few sticks to cook this last meal, and then my son and I must die of starvation" (1 Kings 17:8-12, TLB).

Three challenges presented in this brief encounter between the prophet and the widow match those faced by single heads of household today:

1. How will I be able to provide for my family?

2. How can I serve in the church and still be a good parent?

3. How can I care for my children with my other responsibilities?

Let's consider these questions in light of God's Word.

An Unending Supply

The challenge of providing for children in a single parent home has become a major issue in the United States. Experts project that by the year 2000, it will require two incomes in order for a family to survive the crumbling economy. Financial concerns weigh heavily on the minds of those who must manage singlehandedly.

Single parents are faced with one major question: Will our family survive on my income? Like the widow of Zarephath, you may feel that God has placed unreasonable requirements upon you.

The widow lamented to Elijah, "I haven't a single piece of bread in the house" (1 Kings 17:12, TLB).

How often has this happened in your struggle to feed your family? Do you feel overwhelmed in providing for your children? Take heart! God says to you, "I want you to trust me in your times of trouble, so I can rescue you, and you can give me glory!" (Psalm 50:15, TLB).

Look how the widow responded to the prophet's instruction.

But Elijah said to her, "Don't be afraid! Go ahead and cook that 'last meal,' but bake me a little loaf of bread first; and afterwards there will still be enough food for you and your son...."

So she did as Elijah said, and she and Elijah and her son continued to eat from her supply of flour and oil as long as it was needed. For no matter how much they used, there was always plenty left in the containers, just as the Lord had promised through Elijah! (1 Kings 17:13,15,16, TLB).

The simple act of faith portrayed by the widow's obedience is an example of what God can do for the single parent today. Although the single parent may seem to be "out gathering sticks," God has already made a way.

God's provision can be multi-faceted. He met the needs of the widow, her son, and the prophet at the same time. The widow's God is the same God that you serve today. If He did it then, He can and will do it now!

These same principles apply to your particular situation today. Scripture says the Word of God was "written for our admonition" (1 Cor. 10:11b, KJV). We can learn valuable lessons from the story of the widow and the prophet. Remember that "Jesus Christ is the same yesterday and today and forever" (Hebrews 13:8). If He met the need of the widow then, He will provide for single parents today!

God may prompt you to act in faith just as He called the widow to feed Elijah when she herself was in need. If God asks you to give in faith, He has already provided the means for you to do so. God promises "seed to the sower" (Isaiah 55:10, KJV). He cannot expect you to keep your end of the deal without first providing for you. He must give to you so that you are in a position to obey Him in your giving to others.

A Wise Solution

Elisha succeeded Elijah and inherited the great prophet's mantle of anointing. He too met a needy widow.

One day the wife of one of the seminary students came to Elisha to tell him of her husband's death. He was a man who had loved God, she said. But he had owed some money when he died, and now the creditor was demanding it back. If she didn't pay, he said he would take her two sons as his slaves (2 Kings 4:1, TLB).

Like the widow of Zarephath in the preceding account, this widow bore the primary financial responsibility for her family. Presumably, her bereavement was quickly cut short because of the immediate change of her status from wife and mother to widow and single head of household. She became the sole provider.

This needy widow had two alternatives: either be bitter or place complete trust and confidence in God. She decided to heed the instructions of the prophet Elisha.

"What shall I do?" Elisha asked. "How much food do you have in the house?" "Nothing at all, except a jar of olive oil," she replied. "Then borrow many pots and pans from your neighbors!" he instructed. "Go into your house with your sons and shut the door behind you. Then pour olive oil from your jar into the pots and pans, setting them aside as they are filled!"

So she did. Her sons brought the pots and pans to her, and she filled one after another! Soon every container was full to the brim! "Bring me another jar," she said to her sons. "There aren't any more!" they told her. And then the oil stopped flowing! When she told the prophet what had happened, he said to her, "Go and sell the oil and pay your debt, and there will be enough money left for you and your sons to live on!" (2 Kings 4:2-7, TLB).

When the prophet provided remedies for the situation, she began to trust in the living God for her help. When we trust, we will obey.

Elisha instructed the widow to do specific things, and she did them all.

1. She borrowed without shame. Borrowing indicates a lack. Many single parents don't want others to know about the needs in their lives.

2. She sold the oil regardless of how it might have appeared or what others might have said about where she got it. Often single parents do not lack wisdom to solve problems; however, it is a matter of pride to do as wisdom dictates that leaves most single parents seemingly paralyzed.

3. She closed herself away until her miracle manifested. You may feel lonely, but closeting yourself away in prayer will bring the expected results. Single parents may need to patiently wait for God's provision, but it will come.

A single parent cannot view the economics of the 1990s with eyes void of faith. It is impossible to think of living in the uncertainty of our age without the ever-abiding presence of the Holy Spirit to lead us to the Source.

Service or Busy Work?

Both of the widows we have discussed faced ministry situations in which they had to get involved. The involvement of the widows with the prophets resulted from God's prompting one and the previous status of a deceased husband for the other.

Singles often become very active in many ministries, but some care needs to be exercised in order not to get overextended or to be busy simply to combat loneliness. Some single parents stretch their schedules, thereby inconveniencing their children or delaying the fulfillment of their responsibilities at home.

Time in God's presence will help you to validate activities that are directed by the Holy Spirit and to distinguish between service and busy work. The dangers are obvious. Busy work inevitably becomes unrewarding and arduous, eventually leading you away from the true purpose of God for your life.

Today's single parents can learn a lesson from the prophet. The man of God included the children in the solution to the problem. "Go into your house with your sons and shut the door behind you. Then pour olive oil from your jar into the pots and pans, setting them aside as they are filled!" (2 Kings 4:4, TLB)

Involving your children in the solution guarantees that they will appreciate the value of miracles. Even very young children can learn that God always provides for and blesses the entire family.

Filling the Vacuum

Single heads of households are real people — not just statistics. They must find practical answers to their challenges in life.

Wanting to ascertain the pressing problems they face, I met with a singles group from a church in Southern California. "What are some of your biggest needs?" I asked.

"I would like to have a man around sometimes to help take care of the business. I would like to be able to tell the children that I will refer their particular discipline case to a father. When I walk through the neighborhood and see families sitting down to eat, it makes me want to be able to cook meals for someone else sometimes."

Many other women echoed this same thought. Single mothers spoke openly about their dread of going home alone every night, the misery of planning activities for weekends and holidays, and the challenge of keeping the children entertained.

Single mothers agree that raising sons is no small chore. Women often feel inadequate to be an effective role model for their boys. Their inability to find adequate male role models for their sons only added to their frustration.

How should the Church respond to the many children, especially boys, who are growing up without a male role model in the home? God wants us to be a "father to the fatherless" and a "husband to the widow."

I learned of one case where Christian men stepped in to fill the vacuum in the life of a single parent.

During one church service a single mother stood alone to dedicate her child. The minister asked, "Would any men like to stand with this mother and provide fathering for the child?" One hundred men responded by standing with the mother and her child at the dedication. A few years later the mother married, and her husband adopted the child.

Imagine the impact of growing up with the love and care of 100 fathers. What a beautiful demonstration of protection and provision to the mother, her family, and onlookers.

Unclogging Your Processor

Some of the most productive members of my congregation were single persons. In fact, the single heads of households aggressively poured themselves into a ministry and worked, worked, worked! Despite serving diligently, they still expressed feelings of loneliness, neglect, and inadequacy. Many complained of feeling unwanted even though they were being told that they were appreciated. They had difficulty receiving truth because of previous experiences and attitudes.

Information processing, a mental exercise designed to sort through tons of data, helps us to reach solid conclusions about ourselves and life. When wrong communication, opinion, or data clog this information processing ability, vital truths are blocked from entering. When this happens, decisions are not made based on the solid foundation of truth.

Each of the widows we studied was approached by men of God differently. In both cases, the widows came without preconceived ideas as to how their respective problems would be solved.

Both widows appeared to be unclogged in their processing faculties, making it easy for them to carry out the prophets' instructions. Both women lacked previous experiences that could have potentially hindered them from complying with what was asked of them. They relied on God through His prophets.

Once they understood what was being asked of them, the widows acted and both received the answers they needed. If you are a single parent looking for answers, follow the widows' example. Believe what men and women of God say, and you will prosper and enjoy financial success.

Some single parents would have had difficulty processing Elijah's command: "Bake me a little loaf of bread first" or the one given by Elisha: "Borrow many pots and pans from your neighbors." Most single parents would not have wanted anyone to know what was happening with them. Once information processing undergoes the radical changes that obedience brings, the single parent will have discovered a "new and living way."

And so, dear brothers, now we may walk right into the Holy of Holies where God is, because of the blood of Jesus. This is the fresh, new, life-giving way which Christ has opened up for us by tearing the curtain — his human body — to let us into the holy presence of God (Hebrews 10:19,20, TLB).

This scripture shows how clear processing faculties enable much more effective communication to transpire. Jesus has made it possible for us to trust and obey without fear.

Ministry to Single Parents

What can the Church do to help single parents meet the unique challenges they face? Here are some suggestions:

1. Take a stand against abuse and abandonment. It must firmly oppose wife abuse and child abuse of any kind. In the same way that pastors are charged with reprimanding and disciplining the incorrigible in their flock, they must be willing to do something about men who abandon or abuse their families. The church's involvement will give single parents a sense of security and relieve their feelings of abandonment and helplessness.

2. Create its own Big Brother/Big Sister program. The church should abandon its dependency on social action agencies and become a leader in the area of providing for its community of believers. Innovative and far-reaching endeavors should be enacted quickly to assist single parents with their children.

3. Provide a safe haven. The church must insure that its youth department and singles ministry become a safe place for children and parents to share their heartaches, struggles, and victories. Feelings of embarrassment need to be removed so that parents and children alike can express themselves freely. If their confidence is betrayed, it negates their ability to easily trust again.

4. Organize support groups. Single parents need a place where they can share parenting tips and ideas, such as insight into the behavior of children or dealing with the range of emotions that come with parenting without a partner. Regular meetings would build supportive relationships among single parents and provide much needed encouragement in many practical areas.

Self-image is important. Single heads of household must do everything possible to keep abreast of information, to upgrade parenting skills, and to develop themselves in their career and personal lives. This will keep their self-image high, and success will be inevitable.

Chapter 7

Making It Happen!

Celebration appears throughout this book.

I can hear singles saying, "What is there to celebrate about being single?" If we really understand what celebration means, we can enjoy our season of singleness.

To celebrate implies "the marking of an occasion or event." You are single so why not choose to mark this occasion with a celebration unto the Lord! You are not celebrating the lack of your life-partner but the development and growth afforded you during your single years.

The apostle Paul's words of wisdom can be applied to the single believer today. "I know both how to be abased, and I know how to abound: every where and in all things I am instructed both to be full and to be hungry, both to abound and to suffer need" (Phil. 4:12, KJV).

Paul further states, "Do all things without murmuring and disputings" (Phil. 2:14, KJV).

Do not spend your single life murmuring and complaining. Make the best of it. Celebrate! This is the challenge to the single believer and also to church leadership responsible for the single community.

Church leadership needs to recognize this community of believers as being a very integral part of the Body of Christ. God has joined singles to the Body in a unique manner with unique talents, and He desires to use all of this to His glory!

The apostle Paul declared to the church at Corinth that he was spending time in prayer for them so that they "come behind in no gift" (1 Cor. 1:7, KJV). This same attitude must be exercised when working with a singles ministry in the church.

Singles must be given priority time for the proper development and deployment of their gifts. Scripture states that all believers are "laborers together with God" (1 Cor. 3:9, KJV). A conscious effort must be made to simplify involvement of singles in the general community of believers.

"Many members, one body!" is the motif for involvement, and it must ring in every part of ministry. Singles must know that they are wanted, needed, and welcomed.

Investing in Singles

Churches can consider some of the following suggestions when including singles in ministry. Leaders can open the door of access to singles if they:

1. Invest in singles by systematic development. People need to be reassured that they are valued. No matter how much you tell them that they are loved, they wait for proof. They want to see evidence. Singles not only wait to hear how important they are, they wait to be shown. They need to have the leadership actively working with them to develop their skills, showing them answers to specific questions that may arise during the course of their life in the church.

The Church has begun to see the need for ministry to youth, women, and men. They must also see the need for a strong singles ministry. This recognition involves a willingness to invest in singles. An investment includes finances, time, and creativity.

As a pastor, I discovered that the time and attention I gave to singles helped produce one of the finest communities in our church. At one time, the singles were the greatest financial supporters of the church and the most active in assisting the departmental work. They also demonstrated an aptitude to carry the heart and vision of the church into the community-at-large.

Scripture declares, "For where your treasure is, there your heart will be also" (Matt. 6:21). If the leadership invests time and finances, it sends the rest of the church this message: Singles are important. This is especially true of the senior leader. If he ignores the singles, the whole church will do the same. If he gives them time and attention, the church will consider singles accepted, important, and useful!

2. Include singles in decisions about singles. During the late 1960s, the United States conducted a "war on poverty." Billboards encouraged community participation. One popular poster read, "If you aren't part of the solution, you're part of the problem!"

Singles need to be involved in decisions that affect their lives. The level and quality of that involvement depend on the church and its awareness of the talents and resources in its singles. The formal training that many singles have acquired from institutions of higher learning can be utilized for the kingdom of God.

When I pastored, the singles developed a "core group" concept. The core group, a select group of singles, met with the pastoral staff to plan activities and approaches to the ministry.

Who should be involved with the core group? You'll want to select mature believers who will be examples to the rest of the singles. This committee would meet, discuss, plan, and solicit reactions from the rest of the singles in the church.

Their advisory role helped us to develop activities that maximized participation among the singles. They were an integral part in the planning and decision-making process. This sense of ownership gave success to the programmatic efforts that were carried out through the singles ministry.

Church leadership would benefit by duplicating this concept. Adapt it to your own particular setting, but have your singles involved in their own ministry. Token involvement would be harmful. The involvement must be purposeful and tangible.

3. Consider singles as candidates for church leadership. Eligibility guidelines should be clear for singles desiring to become involved in leadership positions within the church. Singles need to know when they can reasonably expect to be used in the work of the Lord. Many committed singles were unaware that they could qualify for leadership in their churches. Involve them in leadership wherever possible. They will bless the church.

Sociologists suggest that people are more likely to invest time and money where they feel they are making a contribution. For the most part, singles have the same need as others — to make a notable difference in their churches through their personal involvement. Church leaders should tap into this resource of talent and training and channel it toward the building of the kingdom of God.

4. Top leadership should give quality time to singles. The senior minister or lead elder spends most of his time telling the church what is or isn't important. When singles feel secure with the time spent with them, they respond in a positive manner.

The areas that typically flourish in a church are the ones the senior minister gives priority. In the same way, when time is not allocated, those areas die. The senior minister should plan and spend time with all facets of the singles ministry in the church.

5. Assist the singles in forming "joints" in the city and state where the church is located. "Linking" describes what would ideally take place among other singles groups within the city, region, or state. Singles who are exposed to the activities of others will be more encouraged to look to God as a solution rather than toward single's bars and dating services.

Linking should first be encouraged by ministers linking themselves with other ministers in the city, region, or state. The wealth of talent and creativity contained in the singles population will provide a witness to the rest of the Body of Christ. They will see what can happen when people unite.

6. Sponsor an annual singles summit. We organized a weekend summit to discuss all pertinent issues affecting the lives of singles in the church where I pastored. Each component of the singles ministry had workshops and special teachings that accompanied the time away.

During the weekend, a speak-out highlighted the single's time with church leadership. We called it "The Great American Speak Out." Your church can name it anything that you wish. The approach, which is used by highly successful business executives, is rewarding. Let the participants discuss their perceptions of the good and bad points of the singles ministry and the church while you take notes.

I allowed the singles to voice their grievances with the understanding that they were expected to become part of the solution. We created an action list from their input that eventually led to changes and improvements in the singles ministry. Ministers need patience to listen to grievances, but you will gain insight and perspective that will help you plan for the future.

The executive officer of Marriott Hotels holds an annual retreat where managers are encouraged to share the shortcomings of company practices and how procedures can be improved. Although it is difficult for him to patiently listen, he knows the benefits that emerge outweigh his aversion to criticism. Furthermore, the information gathered leads to overall success for the hotels.

The exercise is profitable to both leadership and singles because of the dual role of listening and speaking. The singles listen to leadership when they speak, and leadership listens to the singles when they speak. The results will outweigh your potential discomfort.

7. Remove the "separate but equal" feeling among singles. Statements made from the pulpit and other places of authority give license as to how others view singles. If the pulpit emphasizes married couples and family, the general consensus will be favorable to marriage and negative to singles.

Ministers must check their messages to weed out any comments that might give a negative view about singles or single heads of households. Ministers must let their words be seasoned with grace so that they bless the hearer.

There is not a "single's God" and a "married's God." God is the Lord of both singles and marrieds. Singles should be encouraged to see themselves in the light of God's love rather than looking at life through the shadow of the married population in the church.

Finally, Scripture pictures the Church as a family. Singles should be made to feel as much a part of the family as the rest of the members of the local church. In brief, be a family and include all its members in your activities.

8. *Conduct a check-up every quarter to measure progress.* What obstacles seem to be holding the singles at bay from the family?

• What is happening in the life of the church that might make a single person feel excluded?

• Do the singles in your church know they have a place in leadership and ministry?

• Has leadership effectively communicated to the singles that they are accepted, loved, and appreciated?

• Do comments made from the pulpit hinder the progress being made between leadership and singles? What can be done to prevent alienation?

• Have more singles become involved in the ministry of the church? What is the percentage of increase from the last check-up?

In conclusion, leadership and singles should work closely together to eliminate feelings of isolation and exclusion.

Singles should present themselves mature and acceptable in lifestyle to be eligible for participation in leadership and all other facets of the church.

The affairs of the church should encourage the singles to be a part of the family. A strong emphasis on discipleship should be enacted in the church. A strong discipleship ministry in a local church ensures commitment to the Great Commission. (See Mark 16:15.)

Purpose will not be lost while activities prevail in ministry to singles. A. W. Tozer's impressive statement applies to singles: "Important as it is to recognize God working in us, I would yet warn against a too-great pre-occupation with the thought. It is a sure road to sterile passivity. God will not hold us responsible to understand the mysteries of election, predestination, and the divine sovereignty."[2]

Thus, the value of discipleship. A person can learn what they need to learn in a timely fashion rather than growing too fast with information that will not assist them in the long run.

Tozer paints a picture of an individual who doesn't submit to the wisdom of God: ". . . shallow lives, hollow religious philosophies, the preponderance of the element of fun in gospel meetings, the glorification of men, trust in religious externalities, quasi-religious fellowships, salesmanship methods, the mistaking of dynamic personality for the power of the Spirit."[3]

The spiritual life of a single is first and foremost. They must develop and maintain a growth that will be commendable before God and man. They must ensure that they are secure in what God has called them to do for the kingdom.

Making Yourself Available

What can singles do to make themselves useful to their church? Here are some practical suggestions:

1. Present a life that is commendable to your church. The apostle Paul exhorted Timothy, "Don't let anyone look down on you because you are young, but set an example for the believers in speech, in life, in love, in faith and in purity" (1 Tim. 4:12). The singles should present a life to their church leadership that testifies that they are walking with God. When the leadership sees this, they will be more inclined to use them.

2. Be aggressive in forming friendships within the church. Our church in Southern California grew significantly when our members greeted visitors and made them feel welcome. Our singles led this aggressive attack against unfriendliness. Newcomers who experienced their warmth and sincerity became repeat visitors and eventually members. These new people also began to reach out in friendship. Their new life in Christ affected their own sphere of influence, sparking the growth that occurred in the church.

Our singles operated in the rules of friendship. They suffered long with those who needed it; reached the unreachable and difficult-to-love individuals; and formed small groups that prayed for and supported each other in time of need.

Friendships are hard to make. A person must generally go out of his way to make and maintain friendships. It takes a lot of courage to go from mutual admiration to strong friendships.

A friendship can withstand criticism. It must be strong enough to love a person over the faults you discover in them. True friendship is the antidote for cliques in the church. When people are wrong, friends can tell them that they are wrong and they will hear it. Friends help pastors care for others because they will report missing persons and visit them to make sure they aren't falling away from the Lord.

3. Don't wait to be asked to work in the church. Find something to do and get busy. "No man that warreth entangleth himself with the affairs of this life; that he may please him who hath chosen him to be a soldier" (2 Tim. 2:4, KJV). So much needs to be done in the house of God. Ministers appreciate alert, loving singles who recognize needs and willingly put their hand to the work. Don't wait to be asked. Find a need and fill it!

4. Be visible to your leadership. Submit to pastoral care. Be accountable! Let the pastoral staff know who you are. If nothing in your life hinders you from flowing with the other members, be visible! Keep a high profile. Let the leadership see you frequently.

When I pastored, I noticed that those who weren't walking in total victory became the least visible. Don't pull the prodigal on the leadership. Be alert to their love and care for you.

Meeting the Challenge

Let's review the principles that will assist you in celebrating your singleness unto the Lord. These principles, if applied, can be the stepping stones to achieving a successful single life of excellence unto the Lord.

Principle #1: Understand Your Uniqueness

Accept yourself in Christ with all the unique attributes you possess. You are fearfully and wonderfully made. "I praise you because I am fearfully and wonderfully made; your works are wonderful, I know that full well" (Psalm 139:14).

Principle #2: Value Your Special Selection

Understand your "special selection" and lean on it for your acceptance, security, and self-image. Indeed, God does have a wonderful plan for your life. "Before I formed you in the womb I knew you, before you were born I set you apart . . ." (Jer. 1:5). This enables us to enjoy God's peace not only in the present but in the future. "'For I know the plans I have for you,' declares the Lord, 'plans to prosper you and not to harm you, plans to give you hope and a future'" (Jer. 29:11).

Principle #3: Exercise the Processes of Spiritual Growth and Interdependence

Realize that growth and the development of interdependency are processes. Learn to properly measure your progress toward both. Be honest with yourself, but be fair. Set realistic goals that will build and preserve good character. Who you are is much more important to project than how you look or feel.

Learn to make quality decisions in life concerning your finances and personal development. The quality decision is a decision from which you cannot retreat. The most important decision you can make is to become conformed into His image. "Not that I have already obtained all this, or have already been made perfect, but I press on to take hold of that for which Christ Jesus took hold of me" (Phil. 3:12).

Principle #4: Seek First the Kingdom of God

Gain an understanding of and apply the seek first the kingdom principle to your life, realizing that God is a rewarder of those who diligently seek Him. Learn God's reality about love and humbly defer your hopes and dreams to His wisdom and counsel, believing totally in His faithfulness. "Be delighted with the Lord. Then he will give you all your heart's desires" (Psalm 37:4, TLB).

Principle #5: Discover Your Wholeness in Christ

Identify disappointments in your life and deal with them early so they do not compound later as you face other disappointments and shortcomings. "The Spirit of the Lord is on me, because he has anointed me to preach good news to the poor. He has sent me to proclaim freedom for the prisoners and recovery of sight for the blind, to release the oppressed, to proclaim the year of the Lord's favor" (Luke 4:18,19). "May God himself, the God of peace, sanctify you through and through. May your whole spirit, soul and body be kept blameless at the coming of our Lord Jesus Christ" (1 Thess. 5:23).

Principle #6: Trust in the Reliability of God's Promises

God's ability to produce under impossible situations characterized the lives of Abraham and Sarah. The believer must realize that

God's principle for Abraham and Sarah applies to the unmarried today.

God's promises grow with people. You can never outlive a promise of God! "But Abraham never doubted. He believed God, for his faith and trust grew ever stronger, and he praised God for this blessing even before it happened. He was completely sure that God was well able to do anything he promised" (Romans 4:20,21, TLB). "And I am sure that God who began the good work within you will keep right on helping you grow in his grace until his task within you is finally finished on that day when Jesus Christ returns" (Phil. 1:6, TLB).

Principle #7: Incorporate God's Uncompromising Standards into Your Life

Accept God's standards for Christian living as your own. Never compromise His standards to meet your physical or emotional needs. Answer certain pertinent questions with full assurance:

1. Can I trust God as Isaac trusted his father and Eliezer? (See Genesis 24.)

2. If it is the will of God, can I live as a single person for the rest of my life?

3. Am I living free from sexual bondage now, and will I carry into marriage me as a gift to my partner?

"Wear my yoke — for it fits perfectly — and let me teach you; for I am gentle and humble, and you shall find rest for your souls; for I give you only light burdens" (Matt. 11:29,30, TLB). God provides the grace for us to meet every challenge. "For I can do everything God asks me to with the help of Christ who gives me the strength and power" (Phil. 4:13, TLB). This doesn't happen automatically, however. God requires our cooperation, especially in the area of our attitudes and thoughts. "For people who live by the standard set by their lower nature, are usually thinking the things suggested by that nature, and people who live by the standard set by the Spirit are usually thinking the things suggested by the Spirit" (Romans 8:5, Williams New Testament).

Principle #8: The Principle of Promotion

Singles who desire to be married must learn the principle of promotion. Promotion from a successful life of excellence as a single believer may lead to marriage. For others, promotion may take the form of stepping into ministry or recognizing they are gifted to be celibate.

In another sense, promotion may take the form of celebrating the length of a person's singleness. I do not want to lock a person into marriage as the only expression of promotion.

These principles pose great challenges: a challenge to give yourself totally to God; a challenge to trust Him more than you trust your own emotions; and a challenge to apply principles of godly living as to be conformed into the image of God's dear Son.

You can do it. Single life can be a celebration unto the Lord!

Endnotes

1. *Star Tribune,* Chicago, IL, 11/2/90.

2. A. W. Tozer, *The Pursuit of God.* (Beaverlodge, Alberta, Canada: Horizon House Publishing, 1976), p. 68.

3. Ibid., p. 69.

OTHER BOOKS FROM
Pneuma Life Publishing

Why?
by T.D. Jakes

Why do the righteous, who have committed their entire lives to obeying God, seem to endure so much pain and experience such conflict? These perplexing questions have plagued and bewildered Christians for ages. In this anointed and inspirational new book, Bishop T.D. Jakes provocatively and skillfully answers these questions and many more as well as answering the "why" of the anointed. *Also available as a workbook*

Water in the Wilderness
by T.D. Jakes

Just before you apprehend your greatest conquest, expect the greatest struggle. Many are perplexed who encounter this season of adversity. This book will show you how to survive the worst of times with the greatest of ease, and will cause fountains of living water to spring out of the parched, sun–drenched areas in your life. This word is a refreshing stream in the desert for the weary traveler.

The Harvest
by T.D. Jakes

God's heart beats for lost and dying humanity. The Church, however, has a tremendous shortage of sold-out, unselfish Christians committed to the salvation and discipleship of the lost. This disillusioned generation hungers for lasting reality. Are we ready to offer them eternal hope in Jesus Christ? Without a passion for holiness, sanctification, and evangelism, we will miss the greatest harvest of the ages. God has ordained the salvation of one final crop of souls and given us the privilege of putting in the sickle. Allow God to set you ablaze. Seize the opportunity of a lifetime and become an end-time laborer in the Church's finest hour! *Workbook also Available*

Help Me! I've Fallen
by T.D. Jakes

"Help! I've fallen, and I can't get up." This cry, made popular by a familiar television commercial, points out the problem faced by many Christians today. Have you ever stumbled and fallen with no hope of getting up? Have you been wounded and hurt by others? Are you so far down you think you'll never stand again? Don't despair. All Christians fall from time to time. Life knocks us off balance, making it hard – if not impossible – to get back on our feet. The cause of the fall is not as important as what we do while we're down. T.D. Jakes explains how – and Whom – to ask for help. In a struggle to regain your balance, this book is going to be your manual to recovery! Don't panic. This is just a test!

Becoming A Leader
by Myles Munroe
Many consider leadership to be no more than staying ahead of the pack, but that is a far cry from what leadership is. Leadership is deploying others to become as good as or better than you are. Within each of us lies the potential to be an effective leader. *Becoming A Leader* uncovers the secrets of dynamic leadership that will show you how to be a leader in your family, school, community, church and job. No matter where you are or what you do in life this book can help you to inevitably become a leader. Remember: it is never too late to become a leader. As in every tree there is a forest, so in every follower there is a leader.

The African Cultural Heritage Topical Bible
The African Cultural Heritage Topical Bible is a quick and convenient reference Bible. It has been designed for use in personal devotions as well as group Bible studies. It's the newest and most complete reference Bible designed to reveal the Black presence in the Bible and highlight the contributions and exploits of Blacks from the past to present. It's a great tool for students, clergy, teachers — practically anyone seeking to learn more about the Black presence in Scripture, but didn't know where to start.
The African Cultural Heritage Topical Bible contains:
• Over **395** easy to find **topics**
• **3,840 verses** that are systematically organized
• A comprehensive listing of Black Inventions
• Over **150 pages** of Christian Afrocentric articles on Blacks in the Bible, Contributions of Africa, African Foundations of Christianity, Culture, Identity, Leadership, and Racial Reconciliation written by Myles Munroe, Wayne Perryman, Dr. Leonard Lovett, Dr. Trevor L. Grizzle, James Giles, and Mensa Otabil.
Available in KJV and NIV versions

The God Factor

by James Giles

Is something missing in your life? Do you find yourself at the mercy of your circumstances? Is your self-esteem at an all-time low? Are your dreams only a faded memory? You could be missing the one element that could make the difference between success and failure, poverty and prosperity, and creativity and apathy. Knowing God supplies the creative genius you need to reach your potential and realize your dream. You'll be challenged as James Giles shows you how to tap into your God-given genius, take steps toward reaching your goal, pray big and get answers, eat right and stay healthy, prosper economically and personally, and leave a lasting legacy for your children.

Making the Most of Your Teenage Years

by David Burrows

Most teenagers live for today. Living only for today, however, can kill you. When teenagers have no plan for their future, they follow a plan that someone else devised. Unfortunately, this plan often leads them to drugs, sex, crime, jail, and an early death. How can you make the most of your teenage years? Discover who you really are – and how to plan for the three phases of your life. You can develop your skill, achieve your dreams, and still have fun.

The Biblical Principles of Success

Arthur L. Mackey Jr.

There are only three types of people in the world: 1) People who make things happen, 2) People who watch things happen, and 3) People who do not know what in the world is happening. *The Biblical Principles of Success* will help you become one who makes things happen. Success is not a matter of "doing it my way." It is turning from a personal, selfish philosophy to God's outreaching, sharing way of life. This powerful book teaches you how to tap into success principles that are guaranteed – *the Biblical principles of success!*

Flaming Sword

by Tai Ikomi

Scripture memorization and meditation bring tremendous spiritual power, however many Christians find it to be an uphill task. Committing Scriptures to memory will transform the mediocre Christian to a spiritual giant. This book will help you to become addicted to the powerful practice of Scripture memorization and help you obtain the victory that you desire in every area of your life. *Flaming Sword* is your pathway to spiritual growth and a more intimate relationship with God.

Beyond the Rivers of Ethiopia
by Mensa Otabil

Beyond the Rivers of Ethiopia is a powerful and revealing look into God's purpose for the Black race. It gives scholastic yet simple answers to questions you have always had about the Black presence in the Bible. At the heart of this book is a challenge and call to the offspring of the Children of Africa, both on continent and throughout the world, to come to grips with their true identity as they go *Beyond the Rivers of Ethiopia.*

Daily Moments With God
by Jacqueline McCullough

As you journey into God's presence, take this volume with you. Author Jacqueline McCullough has compiled her very own treasury of poetry, punctuated phrases, and sermonettes to inspire you to trust, love, and obey the Lord Jesus Christ.

Daily Moments With God will direct your thoughts toward God, shed insight on the Scriptures, and encourage you to meditate on life-changing truths. As your spirit soars in prayer, praise, and worship, the presence and power of God will transform you.

Available at your local bookstore
or by contacting:

Pneuma Life Publishing
P.O. Box 10612
Bakersfield, CA 93389-0612

1-800-727-3218
1-805-324-1741